Witnesses to an Execution

PONTIUS PILATE

THE

ROMAN GOVERNOR

The Civil Trial of Jesus

Volume 4

Michael W. Dewar

Published in the United States by:
Dwelling Place Publishers
PO Box 360196
Brooklyn, NY 11236

DPSCleansing.com

ISBN: 979-8-9928854-5-3 (Paperback)
ISBN: 979-8-9928854-4-6 (eBook)

DEDICATION

Dedicated to my granddaughter Lauren. May you grow up to love the love the Lord Jesus Christ with your whole being. May you be guided by His wisdom to make a positive, memorable impact of life, serving the Lord and serving people.

CONTENTS

PREFACE

Welcome to the fourth volume in the series, *Witnesses to an Execution*. Some of you may ask, why this book? And that is a fear question to ask, so let me give you my best answer.

The four evangelists (Matthew, Mark, Luke, John) have given us an authentic and most reliable record of our Lord's birth, death, resurrection, and ascension, but no one gospel tells us the complete story. We must piece it together from all four, and that is a good thing. For sure, three of the four gospel writers were eyewitnesses. Perhaps Luke was not an eyewitness, but he interviewed many eyewitnesses (Luke 1:1-4; Acts 1:1-3).

But I am not trying to chronologize or harmonize the gospels, in the traditional sense, as some have attempted to do. I am just trying to complete the transcript of our Lord's trial in one place by filling in the blanks.

This series is more focused on the last week of our Lord's life, the week of His passion. And the focus of this volume is on Pontius Pilate, the Roman governor and judge who presided over the civil trial of Jesus.

This was the greatest trial of all history, a greatly flawed politician judging One who is Creator, Messiah, Savior, Lord. I think we need a closer look at this judge for two reasons.

(1) He is a compelling eyewitness to the execution of the Christ. And (2) we need to know if this judge was influenced by others, or was he in anyway on the take, as we would say today.

We need to better understand how the prisoner whom Pilate declared innocent, at least three times, of the charge of treason, ended up being executed anyway. That is a scandal in itself!

I intend this book to be an excellent read for the Good Friday and Easter season because it keeps us focused on the passion of the Christ and it fills in some of the blank places in the story. But it is also a book for all seasons, because our salvation which resulted from this mysterious drama is for all seasons.

Like most of my works, this is a small book and is intended for persons in the pews of our places of worship, and for seekers who may not attend church. My hope is that this work will be used for personal and small group study at home, the office, at churches everywhere, and even under some trees in the park.

If you are blessed by this book, I encourage you to share it with a friend, a family member or acquaintance; also give it an honest evaluation on Amazon, or wherever you bought it. Send your feedback to the author, using the contact information on the "About the Author" page.

Finally, I want to thank all of you for your support in getting this series out; it is greatly appreciated!

INTRODUCTION

This book is about Pilate, the Roman governor of Judea, who was the presiding judge at the trial of Jesus of Nazareth. The trial resulted in the execution of the defendant. All this happened in Jerusalem in early first century AD. It was a trial that would make the governor most famous or infamous judge that ever lived, and without doubt the pariah of history.

This book walks you through that trial, showing you where the governor made the right moves, but also reveals the colossal blunder made in the most important case of his life.

Additionally, this work further exposes the nefarious intentions and malignant dispositions of the accusers who brought false charges against the Nazarene and maliciously demanded His execution.

As self-centered and spiritually blind as Pilate was, he quickly sensed some unexplainable, uniqueness about this defendant who refused to defend Himself, a spooky dread that sent shivers up his spine. He wanted to get rid of the case, so he sent the prisoner to King Herod whose jurisdiction the defendant came from. Herod made sport of the prisoner but also sensed the same mystery and quickly sent Him back to the governor.

After interrogating Jesus, Pilate concluded that the defendant was innocent of the charges against Him. Pilate also realized the case was brought out of malice. The next step of justice was for Pilate to release the prisoner and use the Roman Legion on standby to ensure His safety. But the wheel of justice or injustice did not turn that way for the Nazarene that Friday morning.

Instead, the case became convoluted as the judge became sympathetic to the powerful accusers who wanted the prisoner executed. Rather than using the power of his office to render justice, the judge strangely began to negotiate the release of the man he already declared innocent. From here the judge lost control of the case, and things went downhill. At the same time, the accusers mobilized the crowd to shout down the governor to have the prisoner executed.

Then the most bizarre thing that could ever happen in a court of law took place; the judge totally abdicated the bench of judicial responsibility for the case he already declared innocent. The mob decided the outcome of trial, not the judge.

Yet, to reinforce his declaration of innocence for the prisoner, the judge called for a basin of water and washed his hands saying, "I am guiltless of the blood of this innocent man." The accusers and the crowd shouted back, "His blood be on us and our children (Matthew 27:24-25). Justice was aborted and the mob prevailed. The prisoner was executed that day, but that was just the beginning of this innocent man's story.

Innocent blood has a voice that normally cries out to God for vengeance or justice. The (radio) frequency of this voice is heard by God Himself (Genesis 4:8-12). Like the blood of Abel, the blood of Jesus cried out from the parched earth of Golgotha, but for something better than vengeance; it cried out for mercy (Hebrews 12:24).

Other accused who stood before this same judge, vigorously defended their innocence by strong arguments of denial or that they were framed or that their actions were being misunderstood. Those who were guilty plea for mercy or tried to justify their actions by being defiant.

But this man, the Nazarene, did no such things. He was neither disrespectful nor defiant. He had a pleasant demeanor, a calm and serene disposition. He did not speak much, but when He did, His utterance was profound. This is part of the mystery Pilate sensed as spooky (Matthew 27:11-14). A warning from his wife, to have nothing to do with this just man, made the situation even more precarious for Pilate (Matthew 27:19).

Now thousands of years have passed, civilizations have risen and fallen, and the libraries of the world have been furnished with thousands of books about this execution, but the case is as fresh, interesting, and mysterious as the day it happened.

The acceptable verdict is that two hands were guiding what happened on that Friday we now call Good: the hand of an earthly judge, and the hand of the heavenly judge. This book explores these two concurrent realities.

But if that turns out to be true, does that excuse what the accusers of the Nazarene did, and does that excuse what Pilate, the judge and governor did? This book explores these fascinating questions. So, come walk with me through this mystery, where even angels fear to walk. But for us mortals, this revelation is for our edification and blessing. We need to know!

What is even more fascinating, the prisoner that was judged and executed that day, is Himself the Judge before whom we will all stand one day, and that includes Pilate himself.

CHAPTER 1
WHO IS
PONTIUS PILATE?

This chapter answers the compound question, who was Pontius Pilate and why is this book written about him? Pontius Pilate was the Roman procurator or governor of Judea, from 26-36 A.D. in first century Israel.[1]

First, this book is written about him because he was the Judge who presided over the civil trial of Jesus Christ which resulted in His execution by crucifixion. Pilate's encounter with Jesus, made Pilate one of the most famous or infamous persons that ever lived. If this encounter had never happened, chances are, we never would have heard of Pilate. He would have quietly passed shrouded in history like many others.

But now, Pilate is forever enshrined in the creeds of the Church in these words, "He suffered under Pontius Pilate, was crucified, dead and buried."[2] This is a line repeated for centuries by thousands of churches on every continent on earth throughout the centuries.

Second, this book is written to provide a more complete knowledge about Pilate to congregants in the pews of churches across the world, even the one the Lord has made this author overseer. My hope is that with your help, this work will be made available in wide currency to the broader Christian communion around the world.

Pilate, the Man

Much is not known about the early life and family tree of Pilate, except that he was not Jewish. He himself said, he was not a Jew (John 8:35). Furthermore, Ceasar was too shrewd to send a Jew or a Jewish sympathizer to govern a Jewish State. That would have been a disaster waiting to happen. We may not know of Pilate's family connection, but we know of this man's character.

Scholars postulate that his family name "Pontius" suggests that he was connected by descent or adoption to the clan of Pontii (a Roman general). His surname, "Pilatus," a derivative of the word *"pilatus"* which means one armed with a javelin or one who carries the badge of a freed slave.[3] The Scripture, Josephus, and the early Church Fathers are the most reliable sources available on Pilate.

One German legend has it that Pilate was "an illegitimate son of Tyrus, King of Mayence, who sent him to Rome as a hostage." There he committed a murder and was sent to Pontus, where he conquered the barbarian tribes that occupied it, and consequently took the name Pontius. He was later sent to Judea.[4] Of course, this speculative bit is considered legendary.

Some assert that Pilate was a Prefect when he was first appointed to Judea. A Prefect had some administrative duties but was more of a military commander. The title of Procurator or governor was later given. It is further asserted that he was "an equestrian, a title rank of nobility just below the highest level of Roman aristocracy," such as the rank held by senators.[5]

Despite such possible rank, Pilate was not of noble character; he is not celebrated in Roman history. The only documentation there of him in Roman history is a passing reference made by Tacitus that Pilate had Jesus executed (Ann.xv.44).[6] Tacitus may have gotten the information from a Jewish or Christian source.

Some have alleged that the story of Jesus was so unusual and compelling that Pilate must have made an official report to Rome about it. That sounds logical but such report has not been found in the annals of history. The Interpreter's Dictionary of the Bible asserts, "We are bereft of sources that are not Jewish or Christian.[7] Again, what we know of Pilate is from Jewish or Christian sources.

The Character of Pilate

Pilate was no saint or of noble character; he was a brutal man. He had the power of the sword and did not hesitate to wield it with murderous ferocity, to show who was boss. Jesus referenced one such case of his cruelty, when Pilate massacred Galileans at worship, mingling their blood with the sacrifice offered (Luke 13:1-5).

The picture given here is a man who gave orders to his soldiers to invade the place of worship and slaughter the worshippers. When it was over, one could not distinguish the blood and body parts of humans from the animals they were sacrificing to God. It was just one awful, bloody mess, and it speaks of the type of character Pilate was.

Pilate intentionally misappropriated funds from the treasury of the Jewish Temple to build an aqueduct for the city. When people protested his sacrilegious actions, he had his troops bludgeon them.[8] There is also the case of looting the Samaritan's temple on Mount Gerizim, taken the treasure of sacred vessels and murdering a prominent Samaritan official who protested. All this and more happened on Pilate's watch.[9]

Pilate's Political Appointment

Pilate was appointed Procurator of Judea by Tiberius Caesar AD 26. He held the position for five consecutive terms of two years each until AD 36. Some scholars contend that the fact he held the position that long is a testament that he was a successful administrator of Judea. But others will argue that success here is narrowly defined to mean, he kept the tax revenues flowing to Rome and he kept the peace.[10]

Therefore, being successful by Roman standard, does not mean morally good, or successful by Jewish standard and expectation. The Roman worldview was different from the Jewish worldview, one was secular the other spiritual, though at this time corrupted.

Scholars assert that Judea was not considered a place of high priority for Rome to assign a topnotch military brass to control. Since Pilate was not high on the military command, it was a suitable assignment for him to prove himself and become wealthy. The length of his tenure signals that the assignment was right for him, and he acquired personal wealth.

It is further observed that significant political appointments were influenced by bribery, even though bribery was against Roman law and could serve as reason to recall a governor. For example, the position of high priest was a political appointment by the time Pilate took office, but the position was not immune to bribery from the highest bidder.[11]

Judea was a place where messianic zealots were plentiful, and revolutionary groups like the Barabbas movement thrive. These groups could emerge out of the shadows at any time endeavoring to throw off the Roman oppression as Moses did to an earlier empire. This was especially true during Passover season. If the religious leaders were happy and the governor was happy, the chances of things running smoothly was positive.

There was an understanding of cooperation reached between Rome and the Jewish leaders. They were allowed to practice their religion, administer their own laws in the context of the Roman occupation. Jewish leaders were the administrators of their Temple. Most of Jewish life revolved around the Temple and its activities.

Broadly speaking, Rome would collect the tax revenue and maintain the peace. This was a comfortable arrangement for the Jewish aristocracy which were largely priests, elders of the people, and wealthy merchants and landowners.

Overlooking the Temple was Fort Antonia where the soldiers were quartered. They were there to keep the peace, and Pilate could deploy them at any time to put down an uprising.

Pilate had his official residence in Caesarea where the governors lived. But he also had a residence in Jerusalem, the capital city, and would be there in Jerusalem, especially during Passover, just in case there was any trouble.

Passover was generally fraught with messianic fervor, and revolutionary groups would come out of the shadow to attempt another liberation as Moses did to a previous empire. The annual Passover festival was and is the celebration of that first liberation from tyranny under the leadership of Moses (see Exodus 12).

The governor also had the responsibility of trying criminal cases and imposing the death penalty. Jews could try their own religious case and assigned their own penalty as stipulated in the Jewish law. Criminal cases, especially against the Roman State that demanded the death penalty were tried by the governor. But the people who brough such cases to the governor had to bring the evidence also. In the case of Jesus, He was brought by the elite religious leaders of Israel.

The governor also had the responsibility of administering the prerogative of Pardon with the approval of the people. The administration of justice is never perfect, not then, not now. It was not beyond the influence of powerful people, bribery, and nepotism. However, if a Roman citizen were not getting due process, an appeal could be made to Caesar, as Paul did (Acts 25: 10-12, 26:32). The educated, the rich and powerful could always manipulate the system to make it work for them.

This is the man, Pontius Pilate, that Jesus Christ, the Prince of Glory will come before later in this book to stand trial. This chapter is a kind of biographical brief to prepare you, the reader, for what is to come.

CHAPTER 2

MEET THE ACCUSED

Jesus was thirty-three years of age when He was accused by religious leaders of "blasphemy" and "treason" and brought before a regional Roman court for trial. But what is the charge that qualifies Him to appear before this court? He claimed to be a king, and "we have no king but Ceasar" (Matthew 27:11; John 19:15). The Roman court would not accept the case based on the Jewish religious issue of blasphemy, but treason, yes!

But what is the biography of the accused? Many people in the world today know of Jesus, because His story has already circulated for more than two thousand years but to some, He is unknown. This chapter is written as a legal brief for the courts and the press as if His trial were today. People are asking, "Who is the accused, what has He done?" The more known of His innocence will help to ensure due process.

Jesus of Nazareth, also known as the Nazarene, is an itinerant preacher, healer, and miracle-worker from peasant village of Nazareth of Galilee. His mother Miriam or Mary also referred to as the Virgin Mary. But why?

When she was engaged to be married to the carpenter Joseph, before they came together, she was found pregnant. She claimed that she had no intimate relationship with Joseph or anyone else. The child was miraculously conceived after the angel Gabriel brought her a message from God that she would be the mother of the Messiah, Son of God, the Savior of Israel and the world (Luke 1:26-38).

Joseph considered her story incredible and was about to break the engagement quietly, so as not to disgrace her publicly. But as he considered doing that, an angel appeared to him in a dream and confirmed the truth of Mary's claim and encouraged him to proceed with the marriage and he did (Matthew 1:18-25).

Despite many strange events accompanying this child from conception and throughout childhood, no one from among the religious elite took the time to investigate the veracity of Mary's claim or the events associated with this child's life to see if perhaps, He is indeed the long-awaited Messiah prophesied in the Hebrew Scriptures.

For example, on the night of the child's birth in Bethlehem, an angel of God appeared to shepherds on a Judean hillside and disclosed the identity of the child and where to find Him. There was also a choir of serenading angels singing glory to God.

The shepherds immediately left their flocks in search of the child. They found the Christ child in a manger, paid homage to Him, and spread the good news far and wide (Luke 2:1-20). But despite the report of the shepherds, the religious elite of Israel (high priest, chief priests, and elders of the people) launched no investigation to discover for themselves if this child was the Messiah of Israel prophesied in the Hebrew Scriptures.

Sometime later, a caravan of kings showed up in Jerusalem at the palace of king Herod in the dead of night. They were learned men of royal distinction who studied the planetary heavens. They came from a distant land, following a star or comet that signaled to them that a great King was born, and they needed to find Him to pay homage.

They reckoned that a king of the Jews would be born in Jerusalem, in a palatial space, a king's palace. Their arrival in Jerusalem was no small matter. King Herod was taken by surprise and was greatly disturbed by the news. And when Herod is disturbed, that was cause enough for all Jerusalem to be disturbed as well, for Herod was paranoid and fiercely protective of his throne (Matthew 2:1-12). Herod was known for violently lashing out when he felt threatened.

Herod urgently called for the high priest and chief priests to come to his palace in the dead of night. They arrived with scrolls in hand. He inquired of them where this King of the Jews would be born. They searched the Scriptures, found the information and gave it to Herod. They then returned home to continue their sleep, which was so rudely interrupted by this paranoid king.

But Herod, like a fox, quietly dismissed his royal visitors with these instructions: "Go and search diligently for the young child and when you have found him bring me words again that I may come and worship him also" (Matthew 2:1-7). The royal visitors found the Christ child with His mother Mary and her husband Joseph. They worshipped the Child and provided Him with gifts worthy of a King (Matthew 2:8-11).

Then being warned of God in a dream of Herod's nefarious intension to harm the Christ child, the wise men did not return to Herod. They returned home another way (verse 12).

When Herod discovered that he was out foxed by the Wise men, he used the information the religious leaders gave to him in that late night encounter to have his soldiers massacre the children of Bethlehem (Matthew 2:16-18).

But by this time Mary, Joseph, and the Child Jesus escaped the massacre by becoming refugees in another country. By divine direction, they crossed border into Egypt from Hearod's treachery (Matthew 2:13-15). They stayed there until Herod was dead. God directed them to return to Israel; they did, and settled in Nazareth, a town of Galilee (Matthew 2:19-23).

Despite all this revelation concerning Jesus, the Messiah, we have no record of the religious elites of Judaism conducting any investigative search that this child could very well be the Messiah. Their unawakened curiosity is beyond troubling.

Notwithstanding, there were those who knew of the story of the angel appearing to Mary and of her pregnancy. These are people outside of Mary's immediate family circle, but they did not believe her story. They assumed that Joseph was the father, that he and Mary invented the angel story to cover their shame for breaking religious and cultural protocol of intimacy.

This doubt concerning Mary's pregnancy developed into a counter narrative to the truth told by Mary and Joseph. For that reason, the couple lived their lives under this cloud of suspicion concerning the child, Jesus. There are eighteen silent years of Jesus' life that are unaccounted for in the New Testament; God ensured that they are hidden, and for good reasons.

Nonetheless, the cloud of suspicion that surrounded His birth was carried over into His adult life. A group of scribes and pharisees insulted Jesus by saying to Him, "We were not born of fornication; we have one Father—God" (John 8:41).

What do you think they were saying? They were implying that Jesus was born out of wedlock. That is what being born of fornication means. It is an insult equivalent to saying, "You bastard!" They did not believe Mary's story as recorded in the New Testament. Until this day, most Jews do not believe it. If they did, they would have embraced Jesus as their Messiah.

Yet, the story of a virgin giving birth was prophesied in their Bible, the Hebrew Bible (Isaiah 7:14). From Genesis to Malachi the prophets wrote about Jesus but did not use the name because it was not yet revealed. The claims of Mary have strong biblical foundation. She suffered for the truth!

The last we know of the boy Jesus before His adult ministry, is what is on record of Him at age twelve. That would be considered His Bar Mizpah; he became a son of the Law. He went to Jerusalem in a caravan with Mary and Joseph to celebrate the Passover as required by Jewish law.

When the time came to return to Nazareth, Mary assumed that Jesus was with Joseph who traveled with the men, and Joseph assumed Jesus was with His mother Mary, but He was not in their company. They discovered this after a full day of travel. They frantically searched from tent to tent among families and friends, but He was nowhere to be found.

With heavy hearts and blinding tears, Mary and Joseph returned to Jerusalem in search of Him. After a heart-breaking three days of anxiety, they found Him in the Temple among the scholars and teachers asking and answering questions.

Mary said to Him, "Son, why have you done this to us? Look, Your father and I have sought You anxiously!" Jesus replied, "Why did you seek Me? Did you not know that I must be about My Father's business?" But they did not understand the statement which He spoke to them (Luke 2:41-49 NKJV).

His answer to Mary tells us that at age twelve Jesus knew that Joseph was only His step-father. Joseph's business was not the Temple and what goes on there; that was the business of priests and Levites. Joseph was a carpenter from Nazareth, Mary, a housewife. They were surprised by the statement; how could a twelve-year-old boy know that his step-father was not His father and such information was not told to Him!

The religious leaders that this twelve-year-old boy puzzled with His questions and answers should have known that this boy is unusually exceptional. Could He be the Messiah? It appears they never asked that question, another opportunity slipped through their fingers. Think of it, spiritual leaders in the Temple, talking to the Son of God, the Messiah, Savior of the world, and they had no idea. The child grew up to call them *blind guides*.

The Ministry Work of the Accused

Occupation. A person's occupation is important information for the courts to have on the one accused of a crime such as treason. The work a person does can provide leads or insight into his or her character and values, which could impact due process.

In first century Israel, boys would normally take the occupation of their fathers. It is assumed that before His public ministry at age thirty, Jesus took on carpentry, the occupation of His step-father Joseph. But carpentry was not his main mission. He considered the work of kingdom of God, His Father's business, and He was not referring to Joseph (Luke 2:59-50).

When a person is charged with a crime today, we assume that due to strong law enforcement and a well-organized judicial system, the charge is well researched, and is based up a preponderance of the evidence, clear and convincing evidence, or evidence beyond reasonable doubt, and that reasonable justice will be rendered. In ancient Israel, one could be stoned to death under the mouths of two or three witnesses (Deut.17:6-7).

Bearing false witness was a capital crime, a violation of God's moral Law (Exodus 20:16). But by the time Yeshua (Jesus) came on the scene, the priesthood that rendered judicial decision was greatly corrupted, and largely controlled by money, power, and politics. And justice was often perverted or deferred to the rich (See Vol.2, CAIAPHAS: *The Pernicious High Priest*).

Jesus came from the peasant village of Nazareth, not viewed as a place for human flourishing. Prophetically, Jesus was spoken of as a "root out of dry ground, "nothing in His appearance set Him apart from the ordinary Joe (Isaiah 53:2). One Israelite name Nathanel asked, "Can any good thing come from Nazareth?" He was invited to come and see (John 1:46).

In other words, Jesus was perceived by the power brokers as poor and coming from the wrong side of town. So, in the eyes of the elite class, He could never be the Messiah (John 7:50-52). He did not have the pedigree and financial resources to influence policy makers. The religious-political system was tainted with nepotism and bribery, and Jesus would have none of it.

As evidence by His lowly birth, Jesus did not come to curry favor with the rich and powerful or to pay off a corrupted elite to do His bidding. Instead, He confronted them and demanded that they repent. And they hated Him for it and pushed back to silence Him. But His work speaks loudly for Him.

The Character of Jesus Work. Jesus at age thirty began His public ministry. He was introduced as the Messiah of Israel by John the Baptist who baptized Him in the Jordan River (John 1:19-29). At that time, God the Father spoke from heaven, identifying Yeshua (Jesus) as His Son. And the blessed Holy Spirit came upon Him and empowered Him for His mission.

His first public miracle was to turn water into wine, saving a young couple from public embarrassment (John 2:1-12). For the next three and a half years, Jesus preached and taught the good news of the kingdom of God from city to city, in parks, and from mountain sides, sea sides, in synagogues and Temple.

He healed the sick and raised the dead, cast out demons and walked on water. He fed a multitude of over five thousand men, not counting women and children, using a little boy's lunch of two fish and five small rolls. When the feast ended, they collected twelve baskets of broken pieces (John 6:12-13). He fed two other groups after this same order, one four thousand and another seven thousand. He debated His critics on every important subject and came out on the winning side. But that infuriated them all the more to get rid of Him.

Security forces were sent to arrest Him, but they came back empty handed saying, "Never a man spake like this man. He spoke as one having authority" (John 7:45-49). He would not allow Himself to be taken before His appointed time.

The ministry work of the Nazarene can be summarized under three categories of twos: 1) Preaching and teaching about the kingdom of God, 2) Healing and deliverance, and 3) Feeding and debating the opposition.

The Ministry Supporters of the Accused

Jesus' ministry team of twelve Jewish men known as His disciples, were His immediate supporters. They seemed to be arranged in three groups of four in all four lists of the disciples that appear in the New Testament (Matt.10:2-4; Mark 3:16-19; Luke 6:14-16; Acts 1:13). For example, Peter, James, John, and Andrew always appear in the first group, though not in the same order. Peter always appear first in the circle closest to Jesus, and Judas with a few others on the last circle out from Him.

The second group of four is always led by Phillip, Bartholomew, Thomas, then Mtthew. And the third group is James (the son of Alphaeus, Labbaeus (aka sons of Thadeus or thunder or Simon), Simon, and Judas Iscariot. Judas Iscariot appears last always (see MacArthur, *Twelve Ordinary Men*).

There were other dependable supporters of women and men, some of them have financial means. For example, Lazarus and his two sisters Mary and Martha. Mary Magdalene, Susanna, even the governor's wife appears to have been a supporter. Nicodemus and Joseph of Arimathea who stepped out of the shadows when their service was most needed.

Additionally, Jesus commanded a large following of passionate everyday people, who viewed Him as that prophet

Moses spoke about, the Messiah. They received His message gladly because it addressed their everyday needs of life, taught them how to negotiate the challenges of life, and provided them with a hope and a future. There is a spiritual satisfaction that they received that pompous rabbinic homely and empty rituals did not provide.

Here is a man who said, He did not come to destroy the teachings of the Law and the prophets but to fulfill them. He taught and practice non-violence, love for God and neighbor. He terminated old philosophies such as "eye for an eye and a tooth for a tooth," and replace it with turning the other cheek and going the extra mile (Matthew 5:17-48).

Summation

Jesus of Nazareth was a man of the highest integrity, courage, and wisdom. He was a loving, compassionate, non-violent person who was indeed qualified as the Prince of peace.

He was the Master teacher, healer, and miracle worker who served people in love. He properly interpreted the Word of God, and by example lived out its righteousness for all to see. He was indeed the Son of Man and the Son of God.

This is a brief on the accused facing trial in this book before us on charges brought to the court by His enemies. His trial then was not before a jury, but one man named Pontius Pilate. But now you have a chance to sit on the jury and render a verdict that is impartial. All four gospels are submitted as exhibit A, B, C, and D. We will now meet the accusers.

CHAPTER 3
THE ACCUSERS
AND THEIR CHARGES

In the first century AD, Israel was occupied by the Romans, so there were two court systems: Roman and Jewish. And they functioned differently from courts in the twenty-first century. The Roman court was civil and regional; it was the regional authority that rendered judicial decisions be he Prefect, Governor, a King like Herod, or perhaps some other title.

The Jewish court was religious, and decisions were rendered by the Sanhedrin, which was controlled by the priestly class. This Jewish high Council made up of 71 men including the high priest, also had arresting powers and could issue warrants to bring in Jews from other cities for trial in Jerusalem as it was with Saul of Tarsus (Acts 9:1-6).

Whether the court was Roman or Jewish, the accusers would collect the evidence and presented it before the court. In the

Roman court, the case was presented to a judge who considers the evidence and renders a verdict, as we see in the case of Jesus of Nazareth. Judges were not immune to nepotism and bribery.

Often cases were brought for malicious reasons, the evidence tainted, and witnesses manufactured. Even though false witness and bribery were forbidden in Jewish and Roman Laws, it was still practiced. In Israel punishment for bearing false witness was death by stoning. But people with money and power did it nonetheless (Matthew 26:59-60, 28:12-15).

Who are the Accusers?

Jesus is accused of two things: blasphemy as determined by the Sanhedrin where he was already condemned to death (Matthew 26:65-68). The accusers wanted Him dead and could have stoned Him to death as Jewish law demands.

But it was not to their advantage to stone this popular teacher/healer/miracle-worker, perceived prophet to death. Because they run the risk of an uprising from among the common people who benefited most from His ministry. Stoning would have been counter intuitive; just too risky to achieve the desired end. So, they charged Him with treason, a crime against the Roman State. In this case, the Roman governor would be the judge to sentence Jesus to death. But again, we ask the question, who are these accusers?

They are the Jewish leaders, the aristocrats of Israel, which includes the high priest, the seven chief priests, the elders of the people, and most members of the 71 member Sanhedrin. If these people say you are guilty of a crime, furnish a body of evidence, and demand that you be put to death, your chances of being set freed is next to impossible. Because they were not friends of the occupying Roman State. If they can find this Jesus too extreme, it is in the interest of the governor to go along with them.

These powerful men were the accusers of Jesus Christ, and they were certain that the Roman governor would find Jesus guilty as charged and rubberstamp their demand for execution by crucifixion. But it turned out not to be as easy as anticipated.

Why Did they Want Jesus Dead?

There are at least seven reasons why the accusers here wanted Jesus dead, all are drawn from the four gospels, written by men who were eyewitnesses or knew eyewitnesses.

First, the accusers wanted Jesus dead because His popularity with the people threatened their secured and comfortable lifestyle. As already shown, the leaders of Israel had an arrangement with Rome, to continue their lives as they were accustomed without major interruption, providing they met the few demands Ceasar imposed on them, such as paying the tax revenues and maintaining the peace. Crime against the State was the prerogative of the Roman governor with the death penalty.

The religious leaders were allowed to continue practicing their religion, enforce their laws and traditions among their own people, and continue as the administrator of their Temple. This was a comfortable win/win arrangement for Israel and Rome, and a lucrative one for leaders on both sides.

For these reasons, among others, the scribes and pharisees followed the ministry activities of Jesus and concluded that what

He was doing threatened this lucrative and comfortable arrangement and they needed to stop Him (John 11:45-54).

Second, the religious leaders accused Jesus of not keeping the Sabbath, and for not observing the tradition of the elders, or interpreting the word of God correctly. While other teachers quoted their teachers and relied on precedence, Jesus established His own precedence (Matthew 5-7). For that reason, His hears said, "Never a man speak like this man" (John 7:45-47).

Third, they accused Jesus of undermining their legitimate authority and is therefore an imposter. An example of this charge is seen in the interrogation of Jesus by the religious leaders after the cleansing the Temple. They felt Jesus usurped their authority when He disrupted the Temple business and drove out the money changers (Matthew 21:12-17; Luke 19:45-47).

So, they asked Him, "By what authority do you do these things? (Matthew 21:23-27; Luke 20:1-8). Jesus refused giving them the answer they wanted and that further infuriated their anger and strengthened their resolve to killing Him.

Fourth, Jesus made Himself the Son of God and is therefore guilty of blasphemy, a crime punishable by death through stoning. Could they stone a Jew to death guilty of blasphemy? (Mark 2:7; Luke 22:6671;John 18:19-24). Yes, they could, even though Roman law prohibits it. Pilate was not going to intervene if they were stoning one of their own. Stephen was stoned to death for blasphemy without repercussion (Acts 7:54-60).

However, a crime against the Roman State by citizen or non-citizen was a critical matter; it was the prerogative of the governor to judge such case and impose the death penalty by crucifixion. Such cases were without question the governor's responsibility and religious leaders knew that. But they could surely enforce their own law of stoning to death as they were ready to do to the woman, they claimed, was caught in "the very act" of adultery (Leviticus 20:10; John 8:1-11).

Fifth, they accused Jesus of not only disrupting the economy of the Temple but also threaten to destroy the Temple and rebuild it in three days. The disruption spoken of here is Jesus' attempt to cleanse and restore the Temple to its true purpose, a house of prayer for all people, not a den of thieves.

For example, when Jesus said, "Destroy this temple and I will raise it up in three days" (John 2:18-22). As the reference reveals, Jesus was not referring to the Jewish Temple of stone and wood, but the temple of His own body. He meant, if you kill me, I will be raised back to life again in three days. They deliberately took his words out of context and twisted them for nefarious purpose.

Sixth, they accused Jesus of being guilty of false teachings, such as offering His body as meat and His blood as drink in order to live spiritually (John 6:35-60). This teaching was offensive to a Jewish audience who practiced kosher law, because they took it literally. The eating of human flesh and the drinking of blood of any kind is clearly prohibited in the Torah (Genesis 9:4; Leviticus 7:26-27, 17:10-14).

But Jesus was not speaking of the literal consumption of His flesh or the literal drinking of His blood; both were neither legal nor practical. Jesus often speaks in parables, using figures of speech to teach a higher spiritual truth. Jesus was a Jew who came to perfectly fulfill the Law of God, not to violate or abolish it in any shape or form (Matthew 5:17-20).

Jesus is the personified Word of God, the incarnate Word, or the Word made flesh (John 1:1-2,14; 1John 1:1-4). Just as natural bread sustains physical life, *faith and obedience* in and to the personified Word of God gives and sustains spiritual life. Jesus declares that the Evil one comes steal, kill, and destroy but He came that we might have life and have it to the full (John 10:10).

Furthermore, eternal life is embodied in the person of Jesus Christ (John 3:14-18; Romans 6:23). For these reasons, Jesus said, "Man shall not live by bread alone, but by every word that comes from the mouth of God" (Matthew 4:4).

Just as a branch that is connected to a vine draws life and sustenance from that vine, so is the believer in Christ in a spiritual sense (John 15:1-7). Christ is the believer's life and sustenance! Paul, the apostle asserts, "For you are dead, and your life is now hidden with Christ in God. When Christ, who is our life appears, then you also will appear with him in glory (Colossians 3:3-4). In other words, outside of Christ, genuine spiritual life or eternal life is not possible.

The Jews who abandoned Christ during the bread of life discourse failed to make the connection that just as natural bread must enter the body to sustain physical life, the bread of life, Jesus Christ, the word of God must enter our being to give us spiritual or eternal life. They heard the word of God, but they failed to understand it because it was not mixed with faith as Isaiah rightly prophesied about them (Isaiah 6:8-10).

Seven, they accused Jesus of being guilty of using the magic arts or Satanic powers to cast out demons. This accusation is not only illogical, but most disturbing. It is illogical because if Satan cast out Satan, he is working against himself. And any house or kingdom divided against itself cannot stand.

Jesus found this accusation most disturbing, blasphemous, because they assigned the working power of the blessed Holy Spirit to Satan. They were calling good evil, and evil good. Jesus warned them of the danger of committing the unpardonable sin in this accusation (Matthew 12:22-32).

Eight, they accused Him of forbidding paying taxes to Ceaser, claiming to be a king, the head of a kingdom. The preceding seven accusations are religious in nature and have to do with Jewish laws. The Roman governor would not hear such a case much more to condemn a man to death on such charges. The accusers knew this when they condemned Jesus to death before the Sanhedrin, but they needed a charge more compelling to bring the case to the governor.

Therefore, the twin charges of number eight crossed that threshold because they constituted treason against the Roman State. The governor was duty bound to hear this case and render the appropriate punishment the Roman law demanded.

Jewish leaders resented the Roman occupation of their country and the heavy taxation burden. They also loathed their own people who were tax collectors for the Romans. But suddenly, they are now fired up about Ceasar's interests than Ceasar's representative? The hypocrisy is obvious!

They were fired up to bring this case to Plate, because it suited their interest, and they knew the charge of treason would have gotten the governor's attention. They were also sure the governor would have granted the death penalty that they so urgently needed, to get rid this troublemaker from Nazareth.

The fact is, they had malice against Jesus, and they wanted Him dead; that was their real reason for bringing the case to Pilate. They did not stone Him because they wanted Jesus dead a certain way. That is—by crucifixion, because that was the most humiliating and disgraceful way for a Jew to die. In the eyes of Jews everywhere that would show that He was not the Messiah, because He died under the curse of God. Curse is everyone who dies on a tree (Deuteronomy 21:22-23).

But the accusers did not bring with them required evidence neatly packaged to the governor as seen here. Because seven of their reasons had to do with Jewish religious law which Pilate would not concern himself with. However, reason number eight had to do with taxation and treason. This concerns Pilate, even though the accusers were lying on Jesus.

Jesus never encouraged any one not to pay taxes. When His critics wanted to trap Him on the tax question, He held up a coin and asked the crowd whose image and inscription was on the coin. They responded, "Ceaser's!" Jesus said to them, Give to Caesar the things that belong to Caesar and to God the things that belong to God (Luke 20:25).

Because the Passover was so near, the accusers did not have time to fully develop compelling evidence to support their charge of treason. They just pull that rabbit out of the hat with the hope that the weight of the high priest, the chief priests, elders, and the Sanhedrin would be powerful and credible enough to support their claim and demand for execution. Before a Roman court, the rules were different but not above corruption such as bribery, nepotism, and compromised justice.

CHAPTER 4
THE CIVIL TRIAL
OF JESUS

The year is AD 33, a Spring day in Israel; it is the beginning of Passover week. Jerusalem is buzzing with Jews from all over the Roman empire. They are here to celebrate the Passover festival. It represents their liberation from a former oppressive empire, when Yahweh under the leadership of Moses fought against their enemies and gave them repeated victories.

For these reasons among others, Passover time of the year was fraught with revolutionary fervor. There were zealots with their Barabbas-like groups all over the place, trying to make a lucky strike against the Roman State. The governor himself was not safe because he represented Rome, the oppressive empire.

To ensure that the Passover celebration was smooth and uneventful, the Roman governor left his splendid home in Caesaria Marittima, flanked with cavalry and soldiers, and arrived in Jerusalem at the beginning of Passover week. He is here to reinforce the troops stationed here, just in case there was any trouble; there usually was this time of the year.

The troops were quartered in the Antonia Fortress just over-looking the Jewish Temple on a regular basis. The governor's Jerusalem residence, offices and the judgment hall (Praetorium) are also located here. Jerusalem is part of Judea, ruled by Pontius Pilate. King Herod, who governed the region called Galilee, was also in Jerusalem. His Jerusalem residence was a stone throw from the Antonia Fortress, scholars believe.[1]

The Hidden Agenda

The religious leaders of Israel were busy preparing for the Passover festival celebration, but they also had a secret item on their agenda. That was to get rid of this trouble-maker from Nazareth named Jesus, before the feast day. This matter became a priority since Jesus raised Lazarus from the dead and amassed a greater following. At that time a warrant was issued for His arrest (John 11:45-57). But He kept eluding the arresting guards.

On Sunday, the beginning of Passover week, Jesus rode a donkey into Jerusalem ahead of a cheering crowd; they shouted Hosana, to the Son of David, blessed is he who come in the name of the Lord. Hosana, in the highest!" (Matthew 22:1-11). All this caused the Jewish religious leaders increased anxiety. They are afraid that Jesus' popularity may provoke the Romans to Take away their Temple and tightened the noose of oppression on Israel (John 11:47-48).

To make matters worse, Jesus and His parade of followers headed straight for the Temple courts, where He disrupted the business activities of the Temple. He turned over the tables of the merchants and money changers. And He drove out the animals and ministered to the people (Matthew 22:12-17).

When the religious leaders asked Jesus by what authority He was doing these things, He refused to say (Matthew 22:23-27). This heightened the urgency of the religious leaders to get rid of Him before the Jesus movement develops into a confrontation of conflict, warranting the involvement of the Roman military.

The Roman military marching on the Temple court would not be a good outcome for the religious leaders. They must avoid that outcome at all costs. For these reasons and more, they became more determined to arrest Jesus and silenced Him.

However, because of His popularity, it is best not to arrest Him publicly, they reasoned among themselves. It is best to seize him quietly when His supporters are not around. But locating Him was a problem and the feast day is upon them.

It was about this time Judas showed up and volunteered to deliver Him for a price and they were delighted. They counted out to him thirty pieces of silver for the job (Mark 14:10-11). They got an inside man to do their dirty work. Judas knew the schedule of Jesus and all the secret places he conducted classes and had prayer with them.

Jesus was arrested the Thursday night of Passover week under the cover of dark just as He exited the Garden of Gethsemane, where he was praying. The arresting officers and others were guided there by Judas (Matthew 26:47-56).

The arresting officers brought Jesus to the religious leaders who issue the warrant for His arrest. He was tried before the Sanhedrin and sentenced to death on the charge of blasphemy.

They also allowed the soldiers to physically abused Him. They spot in his face, struck Him with their fists, slapped, and mocked Him (Matthew 26:57-60). All this was illegal (see Vol.3).

The penalty for blasphemy in Jewish law was death by stoning. But the religious leaders did not want to do the killing themselves for at least two reasons. *First*, they feared it would cause a riot with the followers of Jesus and by extension attract the Roman military. The military always come with force and the outcome will not be good. And that would reflect on the religious leaders; they would be blamed.

Second, they wanted Jesus to die a disgraceful death at the hands of the Roman, which is by crucifixion. That would make an example of Him and the Romans would take the blame (more on this point later).

The prisoner is condemned to death before the Sanhedrin on a blasphemy charge. But they cannot bring the prisoner to the governor with a charge of blasphemy, because that is a Jewish religious charge. The governor will not hear such a case. These men are not just educated men; they are politically well informed and clever operatives.

Since Jesus did not deny that He is a King, they made the charge, sedition against the Roman State, because there is no king but Caesar. This charge will compel the governor to take the case, and we will prevail on him to have the prisoner executed. This was their way of reasoning.

The Trial By Pilate

Early Friday morning, the day before Passover, the Sanhedrin convened again to fine tune their plans how they were going to have Jesus executed. This early morning meeting helped to legitimize the rushed illegal trial they had the night before.

After they formulated their plan properly, they bound the prisoner and brought Him to Pontius Pilate, the Roman governor for trial (Matthew 27:1-2; Mark 15:1).

The charge of relevance to this Roman court is that Jesus claimed to be King of the Jews. But the accusers had many other charges of no relevance to this court. Marks asserts, "And the chief priests, accused him of many things, but he answered nothing. Then Pilate asked Him, saying, 'Do you answer nothing? See how many things they testify against you!' But Jesus answered nothing, so Pilate marveled" (Mark15:3-4).

"According to Roman law, the refusal to offer a defense, counted as an admission of guilt" (Matt.27:11-14).[2] But Jesus' silence did not mean an admission of guilt in anyway. His silence was the fulfilment of prophecy. Isaiah writes, "He was oppressed and afflicted, yet he did not open his mouth, he was led like a lamb to the slaughter, and as a sheep before his shearers is silent, so he did not open his mouth" (Isaiah 53:7).

Bear in mind that the religious leaders were the accusers and they did not enter Pilate's judgment hall (Praetorium). Why? They considered themselves holy men, so they did not want to defile themselves, rendering them ceremonially unclean to celebrate Passover the next day. Jews do not normally enter a Gentile's residence back then. In their thinking, that would render them unclean. The governor had to come out to them and asked, "What charges are you bringing against this man?" (John 18:28-29).

The accusers answered, "If he were not a criminal we would not have handed him over to you" (verse 30).

Pilate. (assuming this was a religious charge, which would not stand up in a Roman court of law) said. "Take him yourselves and judge him by your law" (verse 31).

The accusers responded, "But we have no right to execute anyone" (verse 31). (By saying that, they revealed their nefarious intent; they wanted an execution because they already determined His guilt.).

Pilate went back inside and put the question to Jesus, "Are you the king of the Jews?" (verse 33). (This is like saying, This is the charge, guilty or not guilty?).

Jesus responded, "Is that your own idea or did someone talk to you about me?" (verse 34).

Pilate retorted, "Am I a Jew? Your own people and the chief priests handed you over to me. What is it you have done?" (verse 35). (Pilate is trying to extract a compelling cause).

Jesus: "My kingdom is not of this world. If it were, my servants would fight to prevent my arrest by the Jewish leaders. But now my kingdom is from another place" (verse 36).

Pilate: "You are a king, then!" (verse 37).

Jesus: "You say that I am a king. In fact, the reason I was born and came into the world is to testify to the truth. Everyone on the side of truth listens to me" (verse 37).

Pilate: "What is truth?" (verse 38). (With that he went out again to the Jewish leaders) and said to them, I find no fault for a charge against him. But it is your custom that I release to you one prisoner at Passover. Do you want me to release, the King of the Jews?" (John 18:38-39). (This is Pilate's first blunder).

He found Jesus not guilty of violating Roman law; he should have set Him free. The release of a prison at Passover is a separate matter but he enjoined it with the current trial of Jesus and asked the accusers approval (His blunder will escalate).

The Accusers Responded (to Pilate's offer of release): No, not him! (they shouted). "Give us Barabbas!" (verse 40).

According to Matthew's account (27:20), "the chief priests and elders persuaded the multitudes that they should ask for Barabbas." Now the crowd is shouting for the seditionist, Barabbas to be released. (The Judge has made a fatal blunder with the case from which he will not recover).

Pilate (made the second blunder). Wanting to please the crowd, he had his soldiers flogged Jesus, hoping to placate the accusers and the crowd and change their minds. He brought Jesus out all covered with blood and said, "Behold, I am bringing him out to you, that you may know that I find no fault in Him" (John 19:1-4).

The Accusers (Shouted): Away with him! Crucify him! Crucify him! (The accuser and the crowd did not change their preference from the release of Barabbas to Jesus).

Pilate (asked the accusers): "What then shall I do with Jesus who is called Christ?" (Matthew 27:22). (He is the judge; he has already determined that the prisoner is not guilty, yet he is asking the crowd what should he do. This is beyond absurd!).

The accusers and the mob (shouted back): "Let him be crucified!" (verse 22).

Pilate: "Why, what evil has He done?" (verse 23).

The accusers: "But they cried out all the more saying, 'Let Him be crucified!'" (verse 23).

Pilate: "When Pilate saw that he could not prevail at all, but rather that a tumult was rising, he took water and wash his hands before the multitude, saying, 'I am innocent of the blood of this just Person. You see to it'"(Matthew 27:24 NKJV). (This is another absurdity; the judge washing his hands does not excuse him from the responsibility to the prisoner before him).

The Accusers: "Then all the people answered and said, 'His blood be on us and on our children'" (verse 24). The religious leaders knew the damning effects of innocent blood, but in their hate for Jesus, they damned themselves and their children.

At this point Barabbas was released and Jesus handed over to the soldiers to be crucified. (The civil trial resulted in a mob decision, nothing short of a lynching). The temptation here is to quickly pivot to say, God's hand was in it. God's hand has nothing to do with this unjust trial. Pilate dropped the ball of justice and he knew it. And he did it for selfish reasons.

Before we look more closely at Pilate's handling of the case, let us go back and look at John's account. We are doing this because we have heavily used Matthew's account.

John provides some interesting nuances. We know for sure that John was personally there. He had an insider's seat from the arrest through the trials, and through the crucifixion itself (John 18:1-16, 19:25-27).

The other disciples fled at the time of the arrest and were hiding. Of course, Matthew (26:56) says, "all the disciples forsook Him and fled" (NKJV). Initially, John may have fled with them, but he knew where the arresting party was taking Jesus and He went there because he knew the high priest and was allowed entrance to witness the proceedings.

Peter did pick up some courage and also followed the arresting party to the residence of the high priest. Having arrived there, John advocated for him, and they let him into the outer court. But shortly after he lost his nerves and ending up denying Jesus (Matthew 26:57-58, 69-75; John 18:15-18, 25-27). So, since John had an insider's view of the religious trial, let's look at some nuance Matthew did not include in his gospel.

John's Account of the Civil Trial of Jesus

The Religious Trial (John 18:25-19: 16). John was known to the high priest and that gave him access into the religious trial of Jesus at the palace of the high priest. John got Peter into the outer court, but not in the inner chamber where he could see and hear the proceedings (John 18:15-18).

Peter, while sitting in the outer court, lost his nerves when identified as a disciple of Christ. He denied knowing the Lord (verses 25-27). This hour of weakness and failure could have ended his apostleship but for the grace of God. He was restored to ministry after the resurrection of the Christ (John 21:15-22).

The religious trial went on until late into the night. They had to adjourn and reassemble early the following morning. At that time, they fine-tuned their plans and delivered the prisoner to Pilate, the Roman governor.

The civil trial (John 18:28-29). Jesus was brought to Pilate at his Jerusalem residence, located in the Antonia Fortress. It was a short walk from the Temple. The high priest, chief priests and elders (perhaps, the full Sanhedrin) that brought Him to Pilate were determined to have Jesus executed.

Pilate took the case because the primary charge was that of treason, Jesus claiming to be a king, when Ceasar was the only king. But that was not the real reason the religious leaders wanted Jesus dead by crucifixion. How do we know that?

The four gospels are replete with the motivation of the religious leaders, but here is the interlocker or the smoking gun, as we would say today. When Pilate declared Jesus to be innocent on the charge of treason and wanted to free Him, the religious leaders strongly objected saying, "We have a law, and according to that law he must die, because he claimed to be the Son of God" (John 19:7). Here the accusers revealed the real reason they wanted Jesus dead (blasphemy).

Note the expression, "by our law." That means, the Torah, not Roman law. The Sanhedrin had already decided the death of Jesus on the grounds of blasphemy (Matthew 26:62-68). And they wanted Him dead, but dead in a certain way, by crucifixion. Why by crucifixion?

They wanted to forever eradicate the belief that Jesus is the Messiah, the Son of God. They wanted Him to die a disgraceful death among criminals on a tree as a false prophet, an impostor. That would show to Jews everywhere and for all times that Jesus of Nazareth was cursed by God. So, He could never have been the Messiah, for the Torah teaches that the person who dies hanging from a tree is under the curse of God (Deut.21:22-23).[3]

The cross was considered a tree. But the Jewish leaders did not know that this time around, hanging from a tree was God's doing for the salvation of all who believe. Christ became a cursed to redeem us from the curse of the law (Galatians 3:13).

Just as their ancestors looked up to the serpent Moses hoisted on a pole and were healed of their deadly snake bites, they in faith can look to Jesus who was hung on a tree and live (John 3:14-16). Jesus would have died on a tree without the wicked help of the religious leaders and Pilate. Their own unbelief turned out to be more damning for them.

These scholars of the Law wanted to humiliate Jesus and make a permanent example of Him. From now on, every Jew can point to the disgraceful way Jesus died and say, see He could never have been the Messiah. That's why they wanted Him dead by crucifixion. But they were wrong in their assumptions.[4]

Again, note that when these priestly scholars of the Hebrew Bible said, "He must die because He made Himself the Son of God." Pilate panicked! The text said, He became even more afraid and went back in the praetorium and resumed questioning Jesus. He asked Jesus, "Where do you come from?" But Jesus gave him no answer. Pilate said, "Do you refuse to speak to me? Don't you realize I have power to free you or to crucify you?" (John 19:8-10).

Jesus replied, "You would have no power over me if it were not given to you from above. Therefore, the one who handed me over to you is guilty of a greater sin" (John 19:11).

"From then on, Pilate tried to set Jesus free, but the Jewish leaders kept shouting, 'If you let this man go, you are no friend of Caesar. Anyone who claims to be a king opposes Caesar'" (verse12). This statement is made to intimidate the governor.

In essence they are saying to Pilate, You represent Caesar, and here is someone trying to unseat Ceasar who appointed you and you want to set him free! What kind of representative are you? You are not a friend of Caesar. Pilate knew if they did not get the execution they were demanding of him, they could easily report him to Rome and have Caesar recall him. With this treachery, Pilate capitulated or caved in to their demands. He handed Jesus over to be crucified (John 19:13-16). The accuser and the mob, inspired by the high priest, the chief priests, and elders of the people, got what they wanted But was justice served? The answer is no; justice was not served.

Pilate's Handling of the Case

As we have shown earlier, the case was delivered to Pilate with the charge of treason. The accusers said that this fellow claimed to be the king of the Jews, and we have no king but Caesar. Plate quickly concluded that Jesus was not guilty of treason. But how did he come to that conclusion?

He asked Jesus are you a king? Jesus did not deny that He is a King. He said, "My kingdom is not of this world. If it were, then My servants would fight, so that I should not be delivered to the Jews; but now My kingdom is not from here" (John 18:16). Let's analyze this statement briefly.

"If my kingdom were of this world, my servants would fight." What servants is Jesus referring to here? Surely not his disciples who fled and were hiding. This is a reference to angels; many scholars missed this. The Son of God is superior to angels; the angels are His servants (Hebrews 1:5-14).

When Peter drew a sword to defend Jesus at the time of His arrest, Jesus order him to put it away. If it were necessary to fight, His Father would put at His disposal "twelve legions of angels "(72,000) Matthew 26:53). Since one angel destroyed one hundred and eighty-five thousand Assyrian's troops in one night, Pilate's Roman Legion would be of no match.

Pilate being a military man himself, saw nothing in Jesus' peaceful demeanor that qualified him to be a threat to Ceasar's kingdom. He claimed no territory and set up no throne. He commanded no army. His followers were mostly peasants, and they were not violent. His kingdom is not of this world. There was no evidence to support the charge of treason against Him.

Again, Pilate left the judgment hall (Praetorium) and reported to the accusers that he found Jesus not guilty of the charge of treason (verse18). The case should have ended here, and the accused released, while the military stand ready to put down any uprising. Had Pilate done that he would not have been the pariah of history that he has come down to be. His blunder has eternal consequences for him, unless he later repented.

So, instead of standing up for Justice, Pilate allowed himself to be hoodwinked, bamboozled, intimidated from doing what was right. He put politics and his own self-interest ahead of justice. And the case went down a slippery slope from here—the judge, knowingly handed over an innocent man to be executed.

The accusers refused to accept a verdict of not guilty as charged. So, they railed on the governor and challenged his loyalty to Ceasar. "If you let this man go, you are not Ceasar's friend, they shouted." Hearing this treachery, the governor knew that these powerful religious leaders had the power to influence Caesar to recall him to Rome and send a replacement.

Few Politicians then (and now perhaps) would risk their position of power and privilege for an unknown man when a powerful majority wanted something else. The governor could not resist the temptation, so he capitulated and handed over an innocent man to be executed (John 19:16).

This was Pilate's final blunder, and it would haunt him for the rest of his life. One day, the role will be reversed. Pilate will stand before this same Jesus at the final judgment to be sentenced for his crimes, not against the State of Rome, but against the Kingdom of God. He will avoid the lake of burning sulfur, only if he had already made his peace with God before physical death came to him.

CHAPTER 5
SUFFERED UNDER
PONTIUS PILATE

The words, "Suffered under Pontius Pilate" appear in the earliest and most important creeds of the Church: The Apostles' Creed, the Nicaean Creed, to name a few. These words not only point to the suffering of the Christ; they give us insight as to how the early Christians viewed and understood the suffering our Lord, and on whom they put the blame.[1]

Bear in mind that the suffering and death of the Christ has a human and a divine side. The human side is under Pontius Pilate, the representative of a government. The divine side is at the hand of God, the head of a government. Both should not be confused. The focus of this chapter is on the human side. And the next chapter is on the divine side. All human perpetrators against the Christ must take full responsibility and bear the consequences for their role in Christ's suffering and death.

Caiaphas, the chief priests, the elders of the people, and most members of the Sanhedrin wanted Jesus dead, and they left no stone unturned until they achieved that end. Yet, they are not mentioned in the creeds of the Church, but Pontius Pilate is. Why is that? This chapter gives the answer.

But the intent here is not to assign blame but to contemplate the redemptive suffering and meaning of our Lord's death. Such understanding, I consider more edifying and fruitful than the empty pursuit of blame. Yet, the historical fact and truth of the suffering and death of the Christ must be told, not covered up.

As Christians, we commonly focus on Christ suffering on the cross leading to His death, but His suffering began before He was nailed to the two pieces of wood we refer to as the cross. And Pilate is infamously memorialized in Christian literature as the chief culprit to be blamed for Christ's suffering and death. Yet, the assignment of blame is not my motivation writing this chapter as already noted. But Pilate cannot be ignored because he was the trial judge who unjustly released Jesus to be executed.

Suffering is a fundamental and troubling part of human life. We are puzzled by it because we cannot comprehend why and how a righteous, benevolent, and omnipotent God tolerates such blight upon His good creation. Suffering is irrational.

Suffering is part of the problem of evil in the world. The problem of evil can cause the best of Christian scholars to stutter, because they cannot satisfactorily explain suffering and evil against the backdrop of a good and benevolent God. Suffering and evil in the world raise more questions than answers. Yet, suffering and evil are real and God is good and loving.

Perhaps, there are more compelling answers to the problem of suffering capsulized in Christ Jesus and His cross that we need to draw upon as we seek to cope with the everyday sufferings of life. The cross was the climax of Jesus' suffering, not just the beginning and the end. In fact, the suffering of the Christ began long b before He was crucified, and the redemptive significance of the cross needs serious and continued exploration.

Louis Berkhof observes that even though Jesus only spoke of His suffering towards the end of His life, "He *suffered during His entire life.*[2] As Christians, we tend to shift and lump His suffering to the week of His passion in general and His death on the cross in particular. But in reality, "His whole life was a life of suffering." "He suffered in body and soul"[3]

The movie, *The Passion of the Christ* was brilliant. But no one can fully capture or duplicate Christ's suffering or adequately explain what He experienced. Nonetheless, this chapter looks at few of the ways He suffered, the best we can.

Christ Suffered Persecution

Every child of God at one time or another suffers persecution; we may take comfort in the fact that Jesus suffered persecution throughout His earthly life, and it began early in His human experience. Parents may draw upon that fact to confort themselves and their children who are experiencing suffering.

In as much as Mary and Joseph lived under a cloud of suspicion concerning the birth of Jesus, we do not know for sure how much impact that had on Jesus teenage and young adult life, because we have no record of His life from twelve to thirty.

We only can assume that as good parents, they protected Him the best they could. Heaven ensures that the information about those years of His life remain classified, perhaps to keep us from unnecessary distraction about His life and mission.

Despite the silent eighteen years of His life to history, some pharisees did not forget the claims of Mary and Joseph concerning the birth of Jesus. They claimed a miraculous conception took place before they came together as man and wife. These pharisees did not believe or forget it. How do we know that?

As an adult, Jesus had frequent confrontations with the Scribes and Pharisees, at times over fatherhood (John 6:41-60). On one occasion, the pharisees ridiculed him by saying, "We were not born of fornication; we have one Father—God" (John 8:37-42). This is not what we would call a Freudian slip; it was a deliberate in your face insult about His conception and birth.

They did not believe the facts of Jesus' birth. And they used their suspicion to humiliate Him. This is a form of persecution when someone tries to perpetuate a lie, a false story to shame and hurt another. Jesus suffered that from the mouths of His own people. By this time the lie was at least thirty years old.

The Sermon on the Mount was spoken early in the ministry of Jesus. In the beatitude section, Jesus add two blessings to those who suffer falsely for Him. The first is, "Blessed are those who are persecuted because of righteousness, for theirs is the kingdom of heaven" (Matthew 5:10). All His adult life Jesus suffered for righteousness, and you will too. When it happens, don't think it strange; it is part of the righteous life.

The second blessing is, "Blessed are you when people insult you, persecute you and falsely say all kinds of evil against you because of me. Rejoice and be glad, because great is your reward in heaven, for in the same way they persecuted the prophets who were before you" (Matthew 5:11-12).

In this blessing, Christ points the sufferer heavenward to a great reward. He also points to others in His service that suffer similarly, Including Himself. So, be encouraged when you are persecuted falsely and for righteousness' sake; it is not gone unnoticed by heaven. In fact, we are told that "all they that will live godly in Christ will suffer persecution."

Christ Suffered Betrayal

Have you ever suffered betrayal by a spouse, a family member, a friend, a co-worker or colleague? You remember the pain you felt in your guts! It was as if that part of your anatomy were going to fall out. That was followed by a sense of generalized weakness, disbelief, depression, then anger and outrage, followed by acceptance and a calm resignation. These emotions are like the stages of grief a terminal cancer patient suffers.[4]

We have all suffered betrayal at one time or another. If you have not experienced betrayal, keep living; it may come sooner than you think. This book is intended to give consolation to those who are going through their *dark night of the soul*. We can all learn from Jesus because He is our supreme example.

Gethsemane was Jesus' *dark night of the soul*. He knew the betrayal was coming because He identified the betrayer at the Last Supper table to the rest of the team (Matthew 26:21-25;

John13:18-30). Verse 21 (of John 13) tells us Jesus was troubled in spirit. He also knew Peter was going to deny Him and told him. But Peter, so certain of his loyalty to Jesus, took it lightly, thinking he could never do such a thing (John 13:31-38).

After the celebration of the Last Supper, Jesus left with His disciples to Gethsemane with heaviness of heart to travail in prayer (John 18:1-2). Judas is gone to wrap up the betrayal deal. Peter, the leading disciple, is standing on quicksand, not fully realizing the severity of what will befall him. At the same time, Jesus is feeling the weight of the cross and the shadow of death closing in on Him. He desired the support of His disciples.

Having reached the garden, Jesus divided His ministry team into two watch groups, the larger group He positioned closer to the entrance. He took with Him Peter, James, and John a little further and said to them, "My soul is overwhelmed with sorrow to the point of death. Stay here and keep watch with me" (Matthew 26:36-38). Note that He shared the depth of His grief with them and requested of them to watch and pray.

He moved on a little further and prostrated Himself, face down on the ground in agony and prayed as never before saying, "My Father, if it is possible, may this cup be taken from me. Yet not as I will, but as you will." He repeated this prayer three times, checking on His disciples in between—He found them asleep, when they should be watching and praying with Him as requested (Matthew 26:39-46).

The fact that he interrupted His prayer more than once to check on His disciples reveals that He was under stress and anxiety, a manifestation of His true humanity. Judas, the betrayer, knew this hideaway, used for prayer and instruction.

Being under Satan's control, Judas would have brought the arresting party directly to this sacred place. Jesus knew of that possibility. But the disciples hardly understood the gravity of what was happening and about to happen. Perhaps, they were still processing what transpired at the Last Supper table and wondering why Judas was not with them. Their lives were about to be completely upended, and they hardly knew it.

Jesus was not alone but He felt alone. We have no record of Jesus asking His disciples for personal help before, but this night was different; He needed their help and asked for it. But they were too tired and exhausted to watch and pray with Him; they fell asleep when He needed them most.

Jesus was in physical, emotional, psychological, and soul agony. He was at the point of death; He said it, "My soul is exceedingly sorrowful, even to death" (Matthew 26:38 NKJV). He felt the weight of betrayal and the weight of the cross. He knew He had to face the betrayer with the arresting party soon.

While he was praying, the man he trusted, mentored for three and a half years, a member of His ministry team, a man He just broke bread with, sold him for thirty pieces of silver. How could Judas stooped so low to pick up so little. Jesus knew what would become of Judas and His guts were falling out in prayer in Gethsemane. In the end, it was Judas' guts that fell out (Acts 1:17-17). (See Vol.*2 Judas Iscariot: The Autopsy of a Betrayer*).

But there is more. Jesus felt the weight of the cross in Gethsemane. For the first time, He felt the full reality of the cross and it scares Him. He explored an alternative way with the Father, but there was none. The way of the cross was the only way to accomplish the work of redemption. So, Jesus submitted His human will to the Father's will.

When I speak of the weight of the cross, I am not talking about the plus shaped pieces of wood. But the weight of the transaction that would take place on Calvary after Gethsemane. It cannot be compared with the crucifixion suffered by the two thieves; their suffering and death were only physical. The unrepentant thief will suffer judgment and eternal hell later.

The death of Jesus is different; it is one of a kind. The sins of all humankind was dumped on Jesus on the cross. He who knew no sin literally became sin for us that we might be made the righteousness of God in Him (2 Corinthians 5:21). Jesus suffered the full punishment for sin upon the cross.

Put another way, Jesus suffered the full wrath of God against sin on the cross (Romans 5:9). He endured the fires of eternal hell in the few hours on the cross. He suffered the separation that a lost soul will suffer in hell. He began suffering all that in Gethsemane and it almost kill Him there. The cup of suffering was so excruciating that He asked the Father for an alternative.

The bloody sweat poured from his body is referred to in the medical science literature as "hematohidrosis." This condition happens when a person is "under extreme stress," resulting in "cold, pale skin, profuse sweating, a pounding heart, and tightening muscles."[5] That's the weight of the cross of which I speak, not the pieces of wood.

The physical suffering of the cross was modest compared to the spiritual suffering that caused Jesus to cry out, "My God, My God, why have you forsaken me!" (Matthew 27:46). Some scholars assert that the anguish of this outcry is akin to the abandonment the lost sinner will experience in hell. Jesus Himself refers to it as "weeping and gnashing of teeth" (Matthew 8:12; 13: 41-43).

Critics of the Christian faith assert that that human suffering is the "Christian's Achille's Heal," because we cannot explain how or why an all-powerful and benevolent God would allow such blight on His creation. Either He is not loving or all-powerful as He said He is, to do something about it.

But on the other hand, John Lennox, Oxford mathematician and Christian apologist, asserts that if that person on the middle cross is really who He said He was—then we must ask, "What is God doing on a cross?" It tell us that God is not alien to human suffering. He is in it with us, and we can trust Him with our suffering. God knows what he is doing.[6] He has scheduled an end to suffering, pain, and death (Revelation 21:1-5).

Christ Suffered Death Threats

Throughout His ministry, Christ was frequently under death threats. But they were unable to kill Him because His time had not yet come. God scheduled the death of His Son to take place on Passover, AD 33, the year He died. Every attempt on His life before that time failed. The time He died was "the fulness of time," the apostle Paul refers to (Galatians 4:4).

Have you suffered death threats at any time? Every one of the apostles of Jesus Christ suffered death threats and more. And many thousands of His followers were martyred as well. Like Jesus, no one can take you out before your time. "No weapon formed against you shall prosper, and every tongue which rises against you in judgment you shall condemn…" (Isaiah 54:17).

God assigns angel to protect His children (Hebrews 1:14). We are told, "The angel of the LORD encamps all around those who fear Him and delivers them" (Psalm 34:7 NKJV). This divine protection does not mean we should become careless and not take reasonable precautions to protect ourselves. At the same time, we should not become paralyzed with fear because that is not the will God concerning us. He wants us to live free and happy. But if we experience suffering, be assured you are not alone; the Lord is in the midst of it with you.

The first death threat against Jesus' life happened when He was a baby. In his attempt to kill Jesus, king Herod macassar the children of Bethlehem. Mary and Joseph had to take precautions by fleeing to Egypt as refugees (Matthew 2:16-23).

Jesus began His public ministry at age thirty, and it appears that He wanted to use His hometown of Nazareth as His ministry base. He returned from baptism in the Jordan River and from a forty-day fast to Nazareth, fully anointed by the Holy Spirit. But His first sermon in His hometown synagogue did not go well. Matthew gives us this intelligence report:

> So, all those in the synagogue, when they heard these things, were filled with wrath, and rose up and thrust Him out of the city; and they led Him to the brow of the hill on which their city was built, that they might throw Him down over the cliff. Then passing through the midst of them, He went His way. (Matthew 4:28-30 NKJV).

These are people, most of which knew Him from boyhood. This is the place of worship He and his siblings attended all His boyhood life with Mary and Joseph. Jesus Himself learned the carpentry trade from Joseph and must have done work for some of them. But now they are ready to take His life because they disagreed with His understanding of the Scriptures.

This behavior repeated itself throughout His ministry from religious folks. For that reason, His relationship with the religious authorities was not good, because they were hypocrites and He was not afraid to call them out. They called Him a friend of sinners, but those were the people that needed a friend.

Christ Suffered Prosecution

Christ not only suffered persecution; He suffered prosecution, false witnesses, and miscarriage of Justice. The justice system was rigged against Him, so He did not get due process.

Prosecution is when other humans use the law to seek redress, punish, put restraint upon, or take the life of another person. In most cases, they claim to be harmed, or that their human rights were abridged by your violation of the law. And for those grievances they are seeking redress, which could be compensation, imprisonment, or even execution.

As we have already seen, Jesus was wrongly arrested and prosecuted for violating both religious and civil laws. On the one hand, He was tried and condemned to death for claims religious leaders considered blasphemous. On the other hand, He was tried for treason against the Roman State, found not guilty, but was executed, nonetheless. That was a grave miscarriage of justice. If it could happen to a righteous person as He was, it can surely happen to anyone of us.

Jesus was hated by the religious leaders who were jealous of Him. The way He lived His life and do ministry threatened their comfortable arrangement they had with the Romans. At least, that was their mistaken thinking; Jesus wanted to make their lives much better. For these reasons among others, the religious leaders constantly sent experts to His meetings to trap Him in His speech.

They asked Him difficult questions such as, whose wife a woman will be at the resurrection if she was married several times? Or who is my neighbor, and is it lawful to pay tribute to Ceasar? All these trick questions, Jesus answered expertly and correctly, putting them to shame. But that made them more determined to silence Him by all necessary means.

Finally, they paid off Judas, a member of Jesus' ministry team, to betray Jesus. With the help of this paid informant, Jesus was arrested at night, false witnesses sought, a false charge concocted, a trial conducted by the Sanhedrin, and a ruling of death resulted (Matthew 26:57-68). All this happened at night which in itself was illegal in the Torah, their own Law.

Early the following morning, the Sanhedrin met again, attempting to make legal what was done illegally the night before. They formulated a plan, decided on the civil charge of treason, and brought Jesus bound to Pilate, the Roman governor for trial and execution (Matthew 27:1-2). These powerful men expected the governor to rubberstamp the execution that they had already decided upon. But it did not work that smoothly.

The governor found Jesus to be innocent of treason and wanted to set Him free. Those who wanted Jesus dead would not settle for His freedom. They pushed Pilate to anger and humiliation until he capitulated. He handed over the man whom he declared innocent to be to be executed.

James Cone, in his book, *The Lynching Tree* equates the cross of Christ to the lynching Black American men suffered in some of the Southern States here in the United States of America.[7] Like Jesus they were innocent men, deprived of justice and found hanging from trees; black bodies swaying in the wind. Both reflect the triumph of hate over law.

Pilate botched the case and robbed Jesus of Justice. There are many followers of Jesus throughout the centuries who were treated the same way. They were denied due process and executed by powerful people. As long as there are judges who can be influenced by power and money, that behavior will continue until "thy kingdom come."

Christ Suffered Physical Abuse

Have you suffered abuse at the hand of a parent, a spouse, a sibling, or the police? These are common sources of abuse in society; people who were assigned to protect you turn upon you. Some abuses are sexual in nature. And they left the victims deeply scared and with a sense of shame and mistrust in people for a long time. Such abuses do not go unnoticed by our Lord, and perpetrators and predators will not go unpunished, though it may appear so for a while. Their day of reckoning and accountability is swiftly advancing; they will not escape.

Take comfort in the fact that Jesus Himself suffered physical by those who should have protected Him. He was abused while in the custody of the religious authorities. Matthew gives us this intelligence report that Jesus was arrested and brought before the Sanhedrin, the seventy-one member Jewish Council, where He was interrogated under oath by the high priest. Not liking the answer Jesus gave to the Council, the high priest declared it blasphemous and guilty of death (Matthew.26:57-64 NKJV).

"Then they spat in His face and beat Him; and others struck Him with the palm of their hands, saying, Prophesy to us, Christ! Who is the one who struck you?" (verse 65). They blindfolded Jesus and struck Him repeatedly, while taunting Him to identify the abuser if He truly had prophetic skills (Luke 23:63 NKJV).

Jesus was also physically abused in the custody Pilate and Herod. Pilate was reluctant to take the case because he knew the Jewish leaders brought Jesus to him out of envy (Matthew 27:18). When Pilate learned that Jesus was from a Galilean and therefore belonged to Herod's jurisdiction, he sent Jesus over to him. Herod was at his Jerusalem residence at the time, perhaps, for the same reason Pilate was in Jerusalem, to ensure order during Passover.

Pilate was governor of Judea and Herod administrator over Galilee. Jerusalem was in Judea where Jesus was arrested. Herod heard of Jesus and wanted to meet Him for some time. He was exceedingly glad Pilate sent Him over, even though the two men were no on good relations up to this time.

The Jewish leaders accused Jesus of many things in the presence of Herod, and Herod interrogated Him but Jesus answered them not a word. He refused to entertain them. "Then

Herod, with his men of war, treated Him with contempt and mocked Him, arrayed Him in a gorgeous robe, and sent Him back to Pilate. That very day Pilate and Herod became friends with each other, for previously they had been at enmity with each other" (Luke 23:6-12 NKJV).

Pilate still maintained that Jesus was not guilty of treason and wanted to release Him. But wanting the Jewish leaders to save face, he had Jesus scourged. Then he could release Him as the prisoner they normally release at Passover. But the Jewish leader rejected that arrangement and called for the release of Barabbas instead, and the execution of Jesus (Luke 23:13-25).

Pilate was humiliated and, in his frustration, caved in to their demands and handed over Jesus to be crucified. The apostle Matthew gives us the following intelligence report:

> Then the soldiers of the governor took Jesus into the Praetorium and gathered the whole garrison around Him. And they stripped Him and put on a scarlet robe on Hm. When they had twisted a crown of thorns, they put it on His head, and a reed in His right hand. And they bow the knee before Him and mocked Him saying, 'Hail, King of the Jews!' Then they spat on Him, and took the reed and struck Him on the head. And when they mocked Him, they took the robe off Him, put His own clothes on Him, and led Him away to be crucified. (Matthew 27:27-31)

The solders had their abusive and humiliating fun, mocking Jesus as King. The irony is Jesus is indeed King, and every knee will bow before Him, and every tongue will confess that Jesus Christ is Lord and King to the glory of God. This will come about at the time and place of His choosing (Philippians 2:9-11).

Christ Suffered to Death on the Cross

The severe beatings Jesus received before the cross was thrust upon Him, left His flesh raw, bloody, and his body greatly weakened from loss of blood. So much so, He fell a few times, according to tradition. The implication is that He fainted. The soldiers had to compel Simon of Cyrene, a husband and father, to carry the cross for Him (Matthew 27:32; Mark 15:21).

The physical abused Christ suffered were extraordinary; it was malice driven. The soldiers were hardened, burly men of war, experts on inflicting physical punishment. Crucifixion was used as a deterrent to would be seditionists against the State.

Jesus had open wounds on his back and all over His body, the spikes from the crown of thorns sunken in his skull, all made for severe pain. All this before the spikes were driven in His hands on feet that held Him to the cross. "Then they gave Him wine mingled with myrrh to drink, ["a primitive type of narcotic'], but He refused (Mark 15:23).[8]

As shown earlier, the suffering of Jesus Christ on the cross was physical, emotional, psychological, and spiritual. The spiritual was the worst. Frankly, it is incomprehensible, because no one has ever suffered like that before or after. The spiritual suffering of Christ on the cross was intended to prevent other humans from that experience in a worse place and for longer.

The sins and iniquities of all humankind were not only dumped upon Jesus Christ, but He also became sin and iniquity. "He who knew no sin was made sin for us" (2 Cor.5:21). During the few hours on the cross, Jesus suffered the wrath of God upon sin, the eternity of separation and abandonment the sinner who rejects God's provision of salvation will suffer in hell. All this is hidden in the words, "whoever believes in Him shall not perish" (John 3:16). The opposite is also true; the unbeliever will perish.

The writing Pilate nailed onto the cross reads, "Jesus of Nazareth, King of the Jews" (John19:19-22) was the charged for which Jesus was executed. It was Pilate who tried Jesus and handed Him over to be executed, and now he nails the charge onto the cross, as the custom was. Pilate did say to Jesus during the trial, "I have power to crucify you, and power to release you" (John 19:10). He exercised his power to take life, not to save it.

Pilate crucified the very person he said was innocent of the charge against Him. It is mind-boggling, but Pilate put political expediency over the life of Jesus Christ. The Church remembers him in its creeds for the coward he was; it says, "suffered under Pontius Pilate." Who was Pilate? The representative of Ceasar's government; he condemned to death the Lord of Glory who is the representative of another government, the Kingdom of God.

Pilate cannot plea ignorance because Jesus did tell him, "My kingdom is not of this world" (John 18:36). Unless Pilate repented of his Crimes against Jesus, the next time these two men see each other, their roles will be reversed. Jesus will be the Judge and Pilate will be facing trial.

Jesus is the righteous Judge who represents another kingdom where the conniving politics of Caiaphas and the corrosive justice of Ceasar have no influence or power.

Summation

This chapter tells of the hands of wicked humans in the suffering and death of our Lord. His suffering was real and comprehensive affecting body and soul. His suffering was more excruciating than the suffering of the two thieves. They were suffering just physical (bodily) suffering, but Jesus was suffering body and soul. In other words, Christ's suffering was also spiritual.

The death of the Christ was a mystery of divine making because not only the hand of man was involved in His death, the hand of God was also involved as you will now see.

The next chapter discussed the hand of God in the death of His Son. Come with me as we walk into this profound, life changing mystery.

CHAPTER 6

JESUS DIED AT THE HAND OF GOD

Jesus suffered and died at the hand of God. The prophet Isaiah speaking of the Messiah 700 years before He died on Calvary said, He was "smitten, stricken of God and afflicted" (Isaiah 53:3-5). This is revolting to our human sensitivity, but God saving us from the bowels of eternal hell is messy business. This is where the mystery of the plot thickens beyond human comprehension. What we know and understand is what God has chosen to reveal through Jesus Christ, the blessed Holy Spirit, and the Word (John 1:1-5, 14; Hebrews 1:1-4).

First, let me say, Jesus would have died at the hand of God, independent of the hand of man. God did not need man's help in providing redemption for the human family. Jesus is "the Lamb slain from the foundation of the world" (Revelation 13:8).

In other words, in the economy of God, the redemption of humans through the Son of God was conceived in eternity but was executed in the fulness of time on Calvary (Galatians 4:4).

Wicked men had their own reason for wanting Jesus dead. God knew the details of their plan from eternity and arranged the death of His Son to coincide with man's plan. But God had nothing to do with their wicked scheme to kill His Son. God did not cause them to do what they did. Unless they have repented, they will bear the consequences of their own sins.

So, let no one blame God for the conniving politics and treachery of Caiaphas and his cronies or Pilate's duplicity of knowingly having an innocent man executed. Both the religious leaders and Pilate, the Roman governor will face the Judgment of God for their role in the suffering and death of Jesus Christ, the Son of God. And let no one excuse their wickedness by pivoting to the saying, "well, it was the hand of God." No! Their doings were the hands of wicked men.

The Uniqueness of Christ Death

Christ did not suffer and die alone; there were two thieves executed beside Him, but His suffering and death was different from theirs (See Vol.1, *The Third Man on the Gallows*).

The two thieves were dying an ordinary death; the method, crude and cruel but ordinary. Christ's suffering and death were extraordinary because it was not just physical; it was also spiritual. Christ was suffering an eternity in hell in those few hours on the cross. The thieves were dying at the hands of men for their own crimes. The penitent thief in his confession acknowledged that the penalty he and his partner in crime received was just, but this just man (Jesus) did not deserve such death as they were receiving (Luke 23:39-40).

The death of Jesus was different. On the one hand, He was dying unjustly at the hands of men for crimes He did not commit. On the other hand, He was dying at the hand of God for the crimes of others (Isaiah 53:3-5). The cross is a scandal.

The Scandal of the Cross

Christ's death on the cross is viewed as a scandalous drama. When you look up the word "scandal" in a thesaurus, it gives the following equivalents: disgrace, shame, dishonor, humiliation, indignity. The death of Jesus Christ was all that and much more.

The apostle Paul observes that the cross of Christ and its message mean different things to different people groups. To the Jews, it is a "stumbling block." A crucified Messiah is gravely offensive to the Jews. Some Jews will spit at the one to mention the name Jesus to them because they consider Him a fraud.

To the Greeks who prided themselves in knowledge and wisdom, the message of the cross is "foolishness." They could not conceive of an all wise and intelligent God deploying such crude and uncivilized method (1Corinthians 1:18-23).

To the Romans who believed in power and glory, a saving Messiah on a cross is not only laughable, but also a demonstration of utter "weakness." Perhaps, that's why they mocked Him with the words, "If you be the Son of God, come down from the cross and we will believe you" (Matt.27:39-44).

The apostle cites the response of a fourth group of people to the message of the cross. He asserts, "but to those who are called of God whether Jews or Greeks, Christ the power of God and the wisdom of God. To this group, the saving message of the cross is the power of God and the wisdom of God. Because the foolishness of God is wiser than men, and the weakness of God is stronger than men" (1 Corinthians 1:24-25).

That the Almighty should become incarnate in the person of Jesus Christ, born in a manger, grew up in a poor, peasant village, lived a humble life, and died disgracefully on a Roman cross, seems too scandalous to associate with an all wise and omnipotent God. But herein lies the explosive, unfathomable mystery of God almighty.

The apostle Paul who understood this mystery, once hidden but now revealed said, "I am not ashamed of the gospel, for it is the power of God that brings salvation to everyone who believes; first to the Jews, then the Gentiles. For in the gospel the righteousness of God is revealed…" (Romans 1:16-17). The gospel is the message of the cross; the good news of redemption.

The Cross as the Work of God

Again, this is where the death of the two thieves and the death of the Christ are vastly different. The death of the thieves were not accomplishing anything beyond paying their debt to society for the crimes they committed. They could receive help from others before they breathe their last breath, but they could not help anybody. One thief asked Jesus for help and received it.

Jesus was accomplishing the work of redemption during His time on the cross, a work that has benefitted billions of humans for time and eternity. The two great works of God are creation and redemption. Calvary is the **Ground Zero** for redemption. Everything God does falls under one of these two categories: creation or redemption. Here, we are dealing with redemption.

Now, we cannot unpack the full mystery of God's work of redemption in this small book, but we can briefly touch on a few important aspects in the rest of this chapter. And note how Christ's death is different from that off the two thieves.

First, *the death of Christ was a sacrifice offered to God for the redemption of the human family*. It was a promise kept and a debt paid to God, the offended party (Genesis 3:15). It is a debt that angels, mortals, or sacrificial animals could never pay but God Himself paid it (John 3:16). Jesus calls His death "a ransom" (Matthew 20:28). A ransom is a price paid for something, or someone held in captivity. This debt was paid by God to God, not paid to Satan. God owes Satan nothing.

Christ's death on the cross is also called a "substitutionary sacrifice." This denotes that Christ did not die for Himself because He had no sins of His own to die or pay for. He died in the place of others. The prophet Isaiah gives us the full scoop of Christ death in chapter 53. But note verses 4-5, "Surely, He has borne our griefs and carried our sorrows. Yet, we esteemed Him stricken, smitten of God, and afflicted. But He was wounded for our transgressions; the chastisement of our peace was upon Him, and by His stripes we are healed" (Isaiah 53:4-5).

Long before Isaiah's prophecy was given, God showed Abraham what substitutionary sacrifice looks like by asking him to offer his son, Isaac, on Mount Moriah, as a burnt offering. At the very last moment, God provided a ram that was offered in Isaac's place (Genesis 22:1-19). This was a prototype of God offering His Son to rescue the human family (John 3:16).

The apostle Paul speaks frequently on this substitutionary work of grace: "For when we were still without strength, in due time Christ died for the ungodly" (Romans 5:6 NKJV). "But God demonstrates His own love toward us, in that while we were still sinners, Christ died for us" (verse 8).

Second, the work of the cross is a demonstration of God's love, justice, mercy, and righteousness. Because God is holy, just, and righteous, He cannot tolerate sin. Sin must be punished. Sin is the violation of divine law, God's law (1John 3:4).

It is evident that from the Garden of Eden, the penalty for sin is death (Genesis 2:16). "The wages of sin is death, but the gift of God is eternal life through Jesus Christ our Lord" (Romans 6:23). Death in this verse means both spiritual, physical, and eternal separation from God (that is hell).

Rather than all eight billion plus humans now living, and all that have ever lived before, and all yet to be born paying the price of death, God paid the price of death Himself through Jesus Christ. He then gifted us eternal life (gift of God is eternal life).

But remember, a gift can be received or rejected. The gift of eternal life is packaged or resident in Jesus Christ (John 3:16; Acts 4:12). And that gift is made available through the gospel. Whoever rejects Christ, rejects eternal life and will pay the full penalty for his or her sins here and hereafter. Through the atoning blood of Christ shed on the cross, we are saved from the wrath of God (Romans 5:9).

The cross then is God's solution to the human sinful predicament, but some ignorant people who think they are more righteous than God, will be repulsed by God sacrificing His Son for our redemption. But know this, God did not force this upon His Son. The Son volunteered for it. Jesus said, "No man takes my life from me, I have power to lay it down and I have power to pick it up again (John 10:11-12).

In other words, Jesus could have backed out of this arrangement at any time, even in Gethsemane. But instead, He chose not to back out (John 3:14-18). If He needed to defend Himself, He could have called for "more than twelve legions of angels" any time (Matthew 26:52).

Again, the Second Person of the blessed Holy Trinity, stepping down to become incarnate was a voluntary act of love, not something forced (John 1:1-4, 14; Philippians 2:5-11).

Third, *God's redemptive work on the cross reconciled the humans to God.* The apostle Paul speaks to this work of reconciliation as follows:

> For if when we were enemies, we were reconciled to God through the death of His Son, much more, having been reconciled, we shall be saved by His life. And not on that, but we also rejoice in God through our Lord Jesus Christ, through whom we have now received the reconciliation. (Romans 5:10 NKJV).

What is reconciliation? It is the work of bringing together two or more parties who were previously at variance or enmity with each other into a peaceful relationship. The relationship between God and the human family was fractured or broken by our ancestral parents' sin in the Paradise garden, then our individual sins. From then, like sheep we all went astray, everyone to his own way (Isaiah 53:6). And the chasm got wider with time. Christ's death on the cross bridges that chasm to a peaceful relationship with God through His Son (Ephesian 2:14-18). Jesus Christ was the God-Man on the cross; as God, He reconciled us to God, and as Man, he reconciled us to our fellow humans. Because of Christ's work of reconciliation, we can both have fellowship with God and with one another (1John 1:5-7).

Again, the work of reconciliation is done by Jesus Christ for the collective human family, but each sinner but personally receive that remedy through Jesus Christ or remain alienated. Once we receive that gift through Christ, we become agents to bring other humans across that bridge. The apostle Paul refers to us as *ambassadors* of *reconciliation* (2 Corinthians 5:18-21).

Fourth, *the redemptive work of propitiation is made possible through the cross of Jesus Christ.* The apostle John refers to the work of Christ on the cross by saying, "He Himself is the propitiation of our sins, and not for ours only but for the whole world" (1John 2:2 NKJV). The NIV renders the word, "propitiation" as "atoning sacrifice." As such, it is not different from "substitutionary sacrifice" discussed earlier in this chapter. The purpose of sacrifice was to atone or expiate the sins of the people, thus shielding them from divine wrath.

But propitiation also carries the notion of covering or mercy seat. It recalls that place between the cherubim, on the cover of the Ark of the Covenant, in the Most Holy Place, where the high priest would once a year to sprinkle blood as he confessed the sins of the people on the Day of Atonement.

Inside the Ark of the Covenant were three things: a pot of manna, Aaron's rod that budded, and the broken tablet of commandments. They represented sin, because they recall three distinct time Israel rebelled against God during the Exodus.

When the high priest on the Day of Atonement apply blood to the mercy seat, the shekinah light of glory would shine from heaven through the two cherubim on the cover of the Ark. It was a symbol that God did not see the sin inside the box because an animal gave its life and its blood was on the mercy seat. Jesus has become the believers' mercy seat or covering; His blood covers us from divine wrath.

Therefore, propitiation (1John 2:1-2) is also saying that the blood of Christ continues to cover the believer who sins. Our heavenly High Priest is appearing before God for us with His own blood. We can "come boldly to the throne of grace that we may obtain mercy and find grace to help in our time of need" (Hebrews 4:16). We have advocate or an attorney to represent us in heaven; He is an officer of the court.

Fifth, Christ's work on the cross "destroys [Satan] who had the power of death" and liberates the children of God from their fear of death (Hebrews 2:14). So, on the one hand, the crucified, resurrected Christ destroys Satan, and the other hand, He liberates the children of God. Did I say, "destroys Satan?"

Destroys Satan. The word "destroy" here does not mean to wipe out of existence but to defeat, to nullify or takes away one's power or authority. Since the crucifixion and resurrection of the Christ, Satan is still alive and well. But his power and authority have been greatly reduced. Any born again, Holy Spirit anointed and empowered child of God can cast Satan out, evict him from any location and run him out of town (Acts 1:8).

The cross was where the Seed of the Woman bruised the head of the serpent, nullifying his power, taking away his authority. The resurrection of the Christ was the full declaration of that victory. The victory announcement of Jesus was two-fold: (1) "I am He who lives, and was dead, and behold I am alive forevermore. Amen. And I have the keys of Hades and Death" (Rev.1:18 NKJV). (2) "All authority has been given to me in heaven and on earth. Go therefore and make disciples of all nations…" (Matthew 28:18-20 NKJV).

The assignment to make disciples, is to free from the dominion of darkness those whom Jesus died for. Satan, death, and hades are no longer in charge; there is no need to fear them.

Sixth, Christ's death on the cross with His resurrection is a declaration that He who fulfills the law and the prophets has taken on the curse of the law upon Himself and has provided atonement from sin for all who believe (John 3:16). "Christ has redeemed us from the curse of the law *because* He was made a curse for us" (Galatians 3:13-14).

As discussed earlier, the law says cursed is everyone who hangs on a tree. Christ was hung on a tree and became a cursed for us that we might become the righteousness of God in Him.

Seventh, the redemptive work of the cross is made effectual and perfect with the resurrection of the Christ. The cross and the resurrection are inextricably bound together; you cannot have one without the other. They are foundational!

The apostle Paul shows us that without the resurrection of the Christ, the work of the cross would have been non-effectual. There would have been no redemption, no salvation. We would still be in our sins and those who have died perish because they would have no hope of a resurrection (1Corinthians 15:12-22).

Jesus by His death and resurrection conquered Satan, death, the grave, and Hades. "Death has no more dominion over Him" (Romans 6:9). Through His death and resurrection, our Lord Jesus Christ has provided all who believe with a hope and a future (John 3:16; Titus 2:11). The cross is the work of God.

Summation

In the economy of God, His great redemptive work was set in motion from eternity past but come to fruition in time on the cross. Bible writer refers to it as the fulness of time.

The death of Christ Jesus is a unique historical event, unlike any other death in history. And his resurrection is unlike any other that was brought back to life, because they all died again but Jesus dies no more. Death has no more dominion over Him.

This chapter shows seven ways Christ's death is unique, standing in a category all by itself. It is the only death that has resulted in a permanent resurrection and has guaranteed the resurrection of all humans (John 5:28; 1 Corinthians 15:22-23).

Two thieves died with Jesus, but what did their deaths accomplish? Nothing beyond paying their debts to society for the crimes they committed.

But the death of Jesus Christ is the second great work of God; it is the work of redemption. The work of God in redemption is greater than His creation works. Redemption costs more and is taking longer. Except for human, God spoke the creation into existence (Genesis 1).

So, creation did not cost God anything. And it ended with a celebration of joy. God asked Job, "Where were you when I laid the foundation of the earth? ...when the morning stars sang together and the angels shouted for joy? (Job 38:4-7).

Redemption cost God the life of His Son and it is taking Him longer. I use the present continuous tense because the work of redemption is going on even as I write this book.

The provision of redemption is over with the cross and the resurrection, but its application is ongoing (Matthew 28:19-20). The Church is tasked with the announcement of the good news (Romans 10:8-15). Slavery is over, emancipation declaration is made, but the slaves need to hear the good news. The slave masters will not volunteer their freedom; Federal troops must compel it. The Church is tasked with that mission (Acts 1:8).

For the believer, the final state of redemption is glorification (Romans 8:29-30). The creation itself must be transformed and brought into the glorious liberty of the children of God (Romans 8:18-25). Redemption is a lengthy, massive, messy, and bloody undertaking. God had to become incarnate to pull it off.

The motivation behind it—God loves his family so much, that He paid the ultima price to save them, and He will see it to the end (Isaiah 53:10-12).God gave the apostle John a glimpse of the finish product for the people of God, and it is breath taking, awe-inspiring. Look for yourself (Revelation 21-22).

CHAPTER 7

WITNESSES FOR
THE DEFENSE

The trial of Jesus was very odd on both the religious and civil sides. There were numerous witnesses for the prosecution but strangely, none for the defense. Yet, both Jewish and Roman laws required credible witnesses for the prosecution as well as for the defense. Due process then demanded credible witnesses; the same is true in modern jurisprudence, credible witnesses are necessary for due process. Was Jesus given a fair trial?

Under Jewish law, two or three credible eyewitnesses were sufficient to stone anyone to death (Deuteronomy 17:2-7,19:15-19; Hebrews 10:28). Women were not used as witnesses in both Jewish and Roman courts, especially in criminal cases; they were not considered reliable. This was the case in most patriarchal societies of antiquity.

Since there were both human and divine hands in the death of the Christ but for different reasons, this chapter will consider the use of witnesses in both the religious and civil trials of our Lord. We will also revisit the hand of God in the death of His Son on the witness perspective.

The Human Trials Revisited

Were there witnesses for the defense at the religious trial of Jesus? This is a due process question. Jesus had two significant human trials, one religious, the other civil.

The religious trial, as already shown, was done before the Sanhedrin by the very people who wanted Him dead. These were the people who accused Him, arrested Him, tried Him, and condemned Him to death for blasphemy. But did not choose to render death themselves by stoning because it was not to their advantage to do so. They wanted Him dead in the disgraceful Roman way, by crucifixion.

There were no witnesses called, to speak for the defense at the religious trial. If the arresting party wanted witnesses to testify for the accused, they had the opportunity to round up all twelve disciples and bring them in to testify for or against Him. But the officers did not bring them in when they arrested Jesus, even though they were all present (Matthew 26:47-57).

The truth was on the side of the accused, so much so that the religious leaders sought for false witnesses to buttress their case against Jesus. Matthew tells us that the "chief priests, the elders, and all the council sought false testimony against Jesus to put Him to death but found none. Even though many false witnesses came forward, they found none. But at last, two false witnesses came forward and said, 'This fellow said, 'I am able to destroy the temple of God and to build it in three days'" (Matthew 26:59-61). They used this testimony, even though it was false. Any member of Jesus' ministry team could have explained what Jesus meant, but the accusers did not care about the truth. They took His words out of context and twisted them to suit their purpose.

So, they accused Jesus falsely before the council, but Jesus did not defend Himself or even worry to explain the false statement made against Him. He remained silent, because He knew He did not stand a chance with these men who wanted Him dead and were just going through this mockery of a trial.

Finally, the high priest took to the floor and put the accused under oath, thus compelling Him to answer a new question, "Tell us if you are the Messiah, the Son of God!" (Matthew 26:62-63).

When Jesus finally answered the question truthfully, they used His answer, as He suspected they would do, to condemn Him to death (Matthew 26:64-67).

Did they ask the accused, "Do you have anyone to testify on your behalf?" No, that question was not asked, if it was asked, we have no record of it. There were two secret disciples on the Council, Joseph of Arimathea and Nicodemus, who were not in agreement with the Council and did not vote to condemn Jesus. To stand up and vigorously oppose this Council of 71 powerful men was to put their own lives at risk.

They were in the minority and would not have made a difference. When their actions could have made a difference, they stepped out of the shadows to claim the body of Jesus and gave it a decent burial. All four gospels record this fact; John includes Nicodemus (Matthew 27:57-61; Mark 15:42-47; Luke 23:50-55; John 19:38-42 NKJV).

The religious leaders were determined to silence Jesus by death, and they wanted to do it when His supporters were not around to start a riot. A riot would move the governor to deploy the Roman Legion to put it down, and that could result in loss of life and perhaps damage to the Temple. The religious leaders would get the blame and be the big losers, so this must be avoided at all costs.

So, to keep Jesus' supporters uninformed, they arrested Him secretly at night and conducted a night trial which was illegal but better than a riot on their hands. By the time news got around to His supporters, the accused would have been crucified or well on the way to His death. That was the religious leaders' calculation. These men were no fools; they were shrewd operators. For more on the religious trial see Volume 3 *CAIAPHIAS, The Pernicious High Priest.*

Were there witnesses called for the defense at His civil trial? The quick answer is no! As shown in previous chapters, the accused was brought bound to Pilate early the next morning for the civil trial. The religious trial had gone into the late night that they had to adjourn and finish up early the next morning (Matthew 27:1-2; John 19:28-29).

Note now, the religious trial the night before was conducted by the Jewish accusers; they gathered the evidence for which Jesus was accused. They were both accusers and witnesses for the civil prosecution. Most of Jesus supporters were still unaware that this was taking place. The crowd gathered at the civil trial to support the religious leaders. Jesus' immediate supporters were His disciples; they were in hiding out of fear.

Where was Judas? He would have made a good witness for the defense, because he had taken back the betrayal money and wanted to rescind the transaction. But the chief priests would have none of that; they would not deal with him. He told them, "I have betrayed the innocent blood." The chief priests knew it was blood money and did not return it to the treasury of the Temple (Matthew 27:3-10). They called it blood money because they knew the accused was innocent.

Even though Judas had volunteered to betray Jesus, the chief priests exploited his greed and lust for money. Judas thought Jesus would have escaped as He had often done in other situations when cornered. If he were at the civil trial, Judas could have told his story and plea entrapment. But he had gone and hung himself (Matthew 26:3-9). But there were others!

Where was Jesus' friend, Lazarus whom Jesus raised from the dead and Lazarus' two sisters, Mary and Martha? They would have made great witnesses for the defense. They lived in Bethany, not far from Jerusalem; someone would have run through the night to tell them. But by the time they round a few friends to get to Jerusalem, the trial would have been over. And even if they did, the bigger crowd for the prosecution would have shouted them down. They were there shouting to have Jesus crucified and the Barabas released.

Where was the bread and fish crowd? Five thousand, four thousand, seven thousand? Where are all the people he healed? Why are there no witnesses for the defense? The most compelling reason has to do with the time-of-day Jesus was arrested and the speed of the trials and execution.

Jesus was arrested Thursday night of Passion Week and the religious trial conducted immediately after into the late night. Early Friday morning He was brought to Pilate for the civil trial. By mid-day Friday, Jesus was already on the cross.

Jesus was not very popular in Judea. He was from Galilee and most of the twelve disciples were from Galilee. For someone to get a message to Galilee to round up a crowd and get back to Jerusalem in Judea, the trial would have been over.

Where was the Palm Sunday crowd? They marched from all over shouting Hosana to the Son of David! They threw their clothes and palm branches on the road, but where are they now to shout for the defense? Again, the religious leaders were clever in plotting the murder of the Nazarene. They ensure He was taken and tried when His supporters were not around, and when Pilate was in conveniently in Jerusalem to sure up security for the Passover Festival. They had Jesus isolated, at least, that was what they thought.

So, Jesus had to be His own defense! But Jesus did not even choose to defend Himself because He knew things His accusers and prosecutors did not know. He was voluntarily giving His life for the redemption of humankind (John 3:16). This brings us to heavenly witnesses for the defense.

God's Hand in the Death of His Son Revisited

Earlier, we addressed the issue of the hand of God in the death of His Son, that the death of Christ was a sacrifice to God for the salvation of humankind (John 3:16). This is basic biblical theology with Old Testament prototype of Abraham, a father, attempting to sacrifice his son Isaac.

In this case, Abraham lifted the knife to slay his son Isaac, but God stopped his hand in mid-air and provided a ram as the substitute sacrifice. But in the New Testament, the knife is in God's hand, and the sacrifice is His own Son, and His hand did not stop in mid-air. He (Jesus) was "stricken, smitten of God, and afflicted" (Isaiah 53:4). The Judgment of God came down on His own Son, even though His Son was innocent of personal sin or sins. He was tempted but without personal sins; He perfectly kept the law of God.

Jesus was not guilty of sin as a state or sin as an act. These are the two ways we humans are sinners: we were born in sin, that gives us a sinful nature, that is a state of being. Because we have a sinful nature, we commit sinful acts. Jesus was not guilty of sin by nature or of sinful acts in this way or any way.

So, from heaven's perspective Jesus was not guilty of a crime for which he needed a trial and witnesses to defend Him. For that reason, He kept silent, and heaven so worked it that no one needed to come to His defense.

Technically, however, we could say, Jesus was guilty of sin but not His own. Note the difference. The Bible teaches that "God made him who had no sin to be sin for us, so that in him we might become the righteousness of God" (2 Corinthians 5:21). Jesus Christ vicariously bore our sins; He took upon Himself our sins and suffered the judgment of God for us.

We must speak candidly and carefully here, less we become guilty of heresy. Jesus took on the sins of the human family and atoned for them. He is our atonement, our substitutionary sacrifice, our sin bearer. He was not placed on trial by heaven as earth placed Him on trial. But He was punished unto death by earth and punished to death by heaven, but for different reasons.

As humans, we all sinned in Adam as well as personally (Romans 5:12). God tried Adam and Eve and promised to send someone to pay the full penalty for the sins of the human family (Genesis 3: 9-19). That promised is in verse 15 as the Seed of the Woman who would come to crush the serpent's head. The cross was the fulfilment of that promise. The apostle Paul writes, "For as in Adam all die, even so in Christ shall all be made alive" (1 Corinthians 15: 22).

At the risk of being redundant, this truth must be emphasized again. Jesus had no sins of His own to pay for. He volunteered to take on the sins, the transgressions, the iniquities of the human family and paid the ultimate price. Isaiah continues, "But He was wounded for our transgressions, He was bruised for our iniquities, thee chastisement of our peace was upon Him, and by His stripes we are healed (Isaiah 53:5).

It must be said once more, God the Father did not force His Son to die for the human family, the Son volunteered to die. And I am glad He did! We owe a debt to God that we could not pay, and God paid that debt in full for us. The apostle Paul writes, "God demonstrates His own love toward us, in that while we were still sinners, Christ died for us" (Romans 5:8 NKJV).

Summation

So, Heaven did not have to put Jesus on trial because He did not commit any crime against heaven or against earth. The religious and civil trials of the Christ were the doings of wicked men; some dressed in priestly vestment to camouflage their treachery. Their mockery was greatly flawed and deliberately dishonest. Both trials were dishonest.

Jesus stood as His own witness before His accusers and chose not to defend Himself. He kept silent most of the time as the prophet Isaiah had long predicted (Isaiah 53:7). He did not need to provide the courts with any witness in His defense, else He would have made it possible, and heaven could have provided security for them to have safe passage.

In terms of bearing witness for Him, heaven had already declared Him to be the Son of God at birth, at His baptism, and on the Mount of Transfiguration (Luke 2:11; Matt.3:13-17; Mark 9:2-8). The Sanhedrin could have asked the shepherds or the Wise Men or those three disciples who were on the mountain that day when God spoke from heaven.

The resurrection of the Christ is God universal declaration that Jesus was exactly whom He said He was. It is also the declaration that God accepted His sacrifice of atonement on behalf of the human family. The sin debt of the human family has been paid in full.

God needed and recruited witnesses for the resurrection. God recruited many witnesses to tell humankind the good news (Matthew 28:18-20; Acts 1:8). Paul tells us on one occasion there were over five hundred witnesses to the resurrection of the Christ (1 Corinthians 15:1-8). Why so many?

Those who wanted Jesus dead also wanted Him to stay dead. For that reason, they paid off the soldiers who witnessed the resurrection and gave them talking points contrary to the truth (Matthew 28:1-4,11-15).

So, there was a false counter narrative being circulated by the enemies of Jesus. But the eleven disciples came out of hiding and became twelve again by adding Matthias to their number and by the *Ascension Day* there were 120 bold witnesses with a global assignment (Acts 1:18-26). On the Day of Pentecost three thousand new witnesses were added to the mix (Acts 2 36-41).Jesus had witnesses where it was more advantageous to fulfill His mission.

CHAPTER 8
PILATE'S QUESTION, WHAT IS TRUTH?

This book is about Pilate, the Roman governor, and his duplicity in the trial of Jesus, the Christ. The book began with Pilate, and we are now ending with him. But why?

Pilate is the most compelling eye-witness to the execution of the Christ. He was the presiding trial judge who found Jesus not guilty of the charge of treason and yet delivered Him over to His enemies to be executed. This is a conundrum that leaves any thinking person dumbfounded; yet not totally inexplicable, in the context of politics and religion.

At least, Pilate was right when he said to Jesus, "Don't you know I have power to crucify you or release you?" The record shows that Pilate certainly had that power and knowingly exercised it to execute an innocent man, to the chagrin of us all.

The most profound question Pilate asked during the trial of Jesus was, "What is truth?" It has come barreling down through history to us. But to our disappointment when the barrel is opened, it is empty. It has no answer to the question, because Pilate walked away before Jesus could answer the question. This is one of the greatest miss-opportunities of all history, a man stands before God and asked, what is truth and did not wait for an answer. Why?

The Irony of the Question

The question is ironic because Jesus said, "I am the truth" (John 14: 4). And He said to Pilate that the purpose for which He was born into this world is to bear witness to the truth. Pilate responded to this utterance by asking, "What is truth?" and promptly walked away before Jesus could respond (John 18:17-8). Again, we ask, why? Why walk away without the answer to such an important question?

We can deduce the answer to this "why" with our own assumptions. First, the casual way the question was asked, coupled with walking away without the answer, signal that the question was sarcastic. Pilate either presumed he already knew the answer, or the answer cannot be known, or the answer was not important, or the truth was not worth hearing to this political leader. His truth was not the truth of this prisoner before him.

Second, Pilate's attitude toward the question he asked shows his skepticism to the subject of truth. It reveals that the truth was not a settled issue for him, and the outcome of the trial he presided over further confirms that he had serious problem with truth. We will consider three views of truth or worldviews that that converged at the civil trial of Jesus, the Christ.

Three Views of Truth

First, *there is the accusers' view of truth.* Who were the accusers and what guided them? The accusers of Jesus were the Jewish high priest, the chief priests (believed to be seven of them), the elders of the people Israel who were all members of the Sanhedrin. The cheerleaders were whatever supporting crowd these leading men could assemble this early in the morning (Matthew 27:1-2; John 18:28).

The accusers were guided by a Torah worldview of truth. But the Torah was diluted by the tradition of the elders, and the priesthood that interpreted the Torah had become corrupted.

The Torah contained the foundational truth that there is one true God, Creator and Lawgiver and He has a people who were assigned to bring His truth to the rest of the world. This they would do most effectively when Messiah comes.

But the people who were given the Torah, isolated themselves as better than the rest of humanity, diluted the Torah by their tradition and rendered the Torah worldview a closed system led by spiritually blind men. They were so blind that the giver of the Torah became incarnate in the person of Jesus Christ, the Messiah but they did not recognize Him. Jesus came preaching pure Torah and they rejected Him and demanded that He be executed. What was wrong with the accusers' view of truth? Often falsehood has a high concentration of truth, and for that reason most people cannot discern the falsehood. The Torah worldview by the time of Christ was corrupted and self-serving.

For the accusers, the truth was what served their self-interest. It masqueraded in clerical vestments, and was reinforced by religious text, and traditions. Their view of truth operated within a closed system and interpreted and guarded by a priestly class.

This view of truth could be most dangerous, because it operated within a closed system, and had blindfolded itself from any other explanations, whether it came from within or without the system. Divergent views were crushed if not approved by the priestly class, even though the priestly class was corrupted. The prisoner who interpreted the accusers' religious text differently and considered those who now accused Him as corrupted.

The accusers who brough Jesus to Pilate had already tried and condemned Him to death for blasphemy. But they wanted the Roman governor to carry out the execution for them. They were convinced the governor would have taken their word at face value and rubber-stamped the execution of the prisoner.

The accusers prided themselves to have the written revelation of God handed down from God through Moses and carefully vetted and preserved by the tradition of the elders. So, even though Pilate found the prisoner not guilty of the charge, they would not accept that. They said, we have a law, and by our law He must die. They had a different standard of truth, a self-serving one. We have a law—the Lawgiver was the prisoner.

Later, we see the same mindset with Saul of Tarsus who was part of this cult. He got his orders from this priestly class who thought they had the corner on truth. The fact is, they are cut from the same cloth as those who will strap bombs on themselves and blow-up innocent people while shouting the greatness of their god. They too have a myopic view of truth.

Second, Pilate's view of truth (the Roman worldview). Pilate was not a Jew and had a different standard or worldview of truth. For him truth was *situational and pragmatic*. On the one hand, each situation is judged and determined according to its context.

On the other hand, the outcome determines the method. If the outcome serves the greater good, then the method to achieve it is of least importance.

Of course, as a political operative, self-interest or self-preservation exerted the greater influence on the decision Pilate reached on the case of Jesus. Pilate was concerned about having an innocent man executed, and he was also concerned about the curse of innocent blood. For the latter reason, he called for a basin of water and tried to wash the curse from him.

But as judge, he had to decide to execute the prisoner or release the prisoner. He could not knowingly execute an innocent man and not the bear the consequences of that decision. No amount of washing will shield him from the consequences of his decision. But Pilate was more afraid of losing his job than rendering justice or the curse of innocent blood.

So, Pilate had the prisoner he ruled to be innocent executed. He made a pragmatic decision that was self-serving. His decision appeased the accusers, and he retained his position as governor but at what cost! In our own pilgrimage of life, at one time or another, we will all arrive at this intersection of doing what is right versus what is expedient or self-serving. The apostle points us to Jesus Himself when he said:

> Do nothing out of selfish ambition or vain conceit. Rather, in humility value others above yourselves, not looking to your own interest but each of you to the interest of others. In your relationships with one another, have the same mindset as Christ Jesus. Who being in very nature God, did not consider equality

with God something to be used his own advantage; rather, he made himself nothing by taking the very nature of a servant, being made in human likeness. And being found in appearance as a man, he humbled himself by becoming obedient to death— even the death on a cross. (Philippians 2:3-8 NIV)

Third, Jesus' view of truth. He sees truth as a quadrilateral or four-dimensional: as personified, as absolute, as universal, as unchanging. This view is adopted as the authentic, Christian worldview. Let's unpack this categorically and briefly.

Truth is personified. Jesus declares Himself as "the way, the truth. and the life" (John 14:6). The definite article "the" that precedes the word "truth" sets Jesus apart as the source of all reality that anyone may identify as true. He is the eternal Word made flesh (John 1:1-5, 14). Verse 14 says, "The Word became flesh and made his dwelling among us. We have seen his glory, the glory of the one and only Son, who came from the Father, full of grace and truth" (NIV).

When you analyze the preceding Johannine quote, you see that truth is also transcendent and eternal; it is enjoined to life in the two passages cited in John's gospel. The apostle John who speaks of the incarnate Word or Word made flesh in the gospel (John 1:1-2, 14) continues his discussion in the first epistle that bears his name. Here he says:

That which was from the beginning, which we have heard, which we have seen with our eyes, which we have looked at and our hands have touched—this we proclaim concerning, the Word of life. The life appeared; we have seen it and testify to it, and we proclaim to you the eternal life, which was with the Father and has appeared to us.(John 1:1-2).

As an eyewitness and close friend of Jesus, John is redundantly expressing a mystery which is almost inexpressible. He uses words of the senses (see, heard, looked at, touch) to show that his experience was not a vision or dream or phantom related but with a real person. The person who said, "I am the truth," "I am the life" (John 14:6).

Human beings have claimed to speak the truth, have the truth, and stand for truth, but none other than Jesus has authentically claimed to be the truth and is not insane. And only Jesus has the credentials to back up such claim. Pilate stood before the truth and asked, "What is truth?"

Truth is absolute. It is a divine principle that stands in a category above everything else. That's why God cannot lie because that would suggest a truth outside of Himself that He is lying about (Hebrews 6:13-18). God cannot lie!

Perhaps, that's why when people swear to tell the truth and nothing but the truth, they raise their hand and ask God for help. To say these words with hand lifted, then lie and engage in a cover up of the truth is damning to the soul.

Truth is universal. The Ten Commandments is a framework of the truth. These ten principles of ultimate truth are the same everywhere. They were intended for the whole human family God made to occupy earth. They came from heaven to earth, so they are true in heaven. Truth is transcendent and eternal.

Truth is unchanging. Truth is the same everywhere. For that reason, the word of God is intended for people everywhere; it is the standard by which life is authentically lived. The word of God tells us who we are and who God is. God is Sovereign, Creator, Lord and Master (Genesis 1-2; Psalm 24:1-2). We are God's off-spring, bearing His image and likeness (Genesis 1:27-28). We are creatures but superior to the brute beast. The very first two chapters of Genesis reveals this clearly.

The word of GodI defines human relationship and responsibility to God; and it further defines human relationship and responsibility to other fellow human beings. The Ten Commandments is the summary or framework that defines or establishes truth (Exodus 20:1-18). The first four commands define our relationship with God, and the six that follow define our relationship with our fellow human beings.

We know that the LORD our God is One, that He is not a created Being, and we must revere His holy name. We know not to embrace or worship any created image as God, whether formed by us or anyone else. To do so is idolatry, lies of the highest order, that carries the penalty of death (Exodus 20:1-11).

Six of the commands define our relationship and responsibility to our fellow humans or neighbors (Exodus 20:12-17). They teach us that not only our relationship with God is sacred as shown in the first four commands, but our relationship with other humans is also sacred. Therefore, we respect and honor parents. We do not take the life of other humans, because like us, they are image bearers of God. We respect our neighbors' property, so we do not covet or steal them. We do not lie or bear false witness against anyone because that perverts justice and peaceful coexistence.

The Ten Commands are not suggestions to be ignored; they are Divine Executive Orders, truths to obey. Therefore, idolatry, adultery, murder, coveting, stealing, lying, and bearing false witness are wrong because they depart from God established truth. Violation constitutes defiance of the law and the Lawgiver.

Violation of these commands fractures the sacred trust between the Creator and creature and between humans. These divine commands are applicable everywhere and anywhere; they are universal truths. They are revealed everywhere, but not practiced everywhere, because they are suppressed by sinful human nature (Romans 1:18-24). But every society on earth, to one degree or another, embrace elements of these truths, otherwise civil society would be impossible. It is for these reasons that the personified truth became incarnate (John 1:14).

Did Pilate Know Jesus?

Pilate did not know or even acquainted with Jesus; he had no relationship with Jesus before that day. Jesus was brought to him as a prisoner. Yet, Jesus was the answer to the question that Pilate asked (What is truth?). But Pilate did not really want to know the answer; otherwise, he would have waited for it. The question was his sarcastic response to something Jesus had said.

However, by interrogating Jesus on the charge of treason, Pilate arrived at the truth that Jesus was not guilty of the charge, though not at the truth of His personhood. Pilate repeated that conclusion of Jesus innocence at least three times, and he did not change his position on the innocence of Jesus. He went as far as washing his hands from the curse of sheading innocent blood, but not far enough to release Jesus.

Wanting to appease the powerful religious leaders and preserve his governorship, Pilate handed over the man he declared innocent to be executed. This is an example of suppressing or ignoring the truth. The truth was not worth defending. If a judge cannot defend the truth, he has no business serving as judge. By not being guided by the truth he knew, like Judas, Pilate damned himself (if he didn't repent). He could have avoided becoming another pariah of history.

Knowing Jesus

Earlier, I stated that Pilate did not know or had any acquaintance with Jesus prior to the day Jesus was brought to him as a prisoner. By interrogation, Pilate arrived at the truth that Jesus was not guilty of the charge of treason. But Pilate still did not know the personhood of Jesus, who He was in terms of being Messiah, Savior, Son of God.

Even if Pilate heard these terms, they would have meant nothing to him. This level of knowing or enlightenment about Jesus comes only through divine revelation, as it was with Peter in Caesaria Phillippi some time earlier (Matthew 16:13-16). In that case, Jesus asked His disciples, "Who do people say that I am?" They replied, "Some say, you are John the Baptist, Elijah, Jeremiah or another prophet." Jesus then asked them, "Who do you say that I am?" Peter blurted out, "You are the Christ, Son of the Living God." Jesus said to Peter, "Flesh and blood did not reveal that to you, but my Father in heaven."

In other words, without a direct revelation from God, Pilate could not have known that the prisoner before him was the Mesiah, Savior, Son of God. Even if he were told, he would not have known what that meant. He would have walked away saying, Son of God, ha! Same as he did when he said, What is truth? And walked away.

The accusers, Jewish religious leaders who brought Jesus to Pilate should have known, because they had the written revelation of God in which the Messiah was revealed. But they failed to recognized Him as such or they did not care. So, it is not surprising that Pilate who was not a Jew did not recognize Him either. Pilate was not looking for a Messiah and would not have recognized one. Personified truth in this context is only known by revelation. But as a judge he should have abided by the truth of innocence that he arrived at by judicial investigation. But he did not; he suppressed the truth for political expediency.

Lessons Learned

Pilate lived in the early first century AD, a politician operating in a pre-Christian environment with limited revelation about God. We are living in the 21st century with over two thousand years of Christian enlightenment. But are we any better than Pilate in our response to truth? Are we any better than the Jewish religious leaders who with torah in hand, gave Herod the information about the identity of the Christ child and went back to bed to sleep as usual? And now handed over their Messiah to Pilate, and demanded that He be executed on their terms?

Look again at politics and religion in America. Church going, Bible quoting people, who know the truth but often look the other way for the same reason as Pilate: self-interest and political expediency. We have the written truth of God's word in hand, even take solemn oaths with raised hand in His name, but forget them shortly after. We listen to the spoken word preached from thousands of pulpits every Sunday, and we claim to have a relationship with the personified truth, Jesus Christ.

But are we any better than Pilate who practiced the corrosive politics of Caesar and conniving, hypocritical values of Caiaphas? Are we at the same intersection as Pilate, standing before Jesus asking, "What is truth?" Jesus once asked his disciples, "Who do people are saying that I am?" They gave this report, "Some say, 'You are Jeremiah, 'Elijah, 'John the Baptist come back to life, or one of the prophets'" (Matthew 16:13-14).

Jesus then asked them, "But who do you say that I am?" Peter blurted out, "You are the Christ, the Son of the Living God." Jesus said, you are right Peter but that was a revelation given to you from "my Father in heaven" (verses 15-17).

The day is coming when all humankind on bended knees will acknowledge and confess that Jesus Christ is the Son of God, Savior, and Lord (Philip.2:9-11). If Pilate did not do so before he died, he will do so at the coming judgment. We either bow and confess now or later. Putting it off for later is dangerous, do it now (Romans 10:9-10).

REFERENCES

Chapter 1

1. Unger, Merrill F. *The New Unger's Bible Dictionary*. R.K. Harrison, Editor. Chicago, IL: Moody Bible Institute, 1988, 1009.

2. Holcomb, Justin S. Know the Creeds and Councils. Grand Rapids, MI: Zondervan, 2024. 27 (The Apostle' Creed).

3. Unger's, 1009

4. *Ibid.*

5. Constantinou, Eugenia Scarvelis, PhD. *The Crucifixion of the King of Glory*. Chesterton IN Ancient Faith Publishing, 2021, 163.

6. Flavius, Josephus. *The Works of Josephus*. Translated by William Whiston. Peabody, MA: Hendrickson Publishers, 1987.

7. Buttrick, George Arthur. Editor. *The Interpreters' Dictionary of the Bible*. Vol. k-Q. Nashville, TN: Abingdon Press, 1962, 811.

8. *Ibid.*

9. *Ibid.*

10. The New Unger's Dictionary of the Bible, 1009

11. *The Crucifixion of the King of Glory*, 164

Chapter 4

1. *The Crucifixion of the King of Glory,161.*
2. *Holman Study Bible NKJV Edition.* Footnotes on Matthew 27:11-14. Nashville, TN: Holman Publishers, 2015,1649.
3. *The Crucifixion of the King of Glory,* **214-222.**
4. *Ibid.*

Chapter 5

1. Holcomb, Justin S. Know the Creeds and Councils. Grand Rapids, MI: Zondervan, 2024. 27 (The Apostle' Creed).
2. Berkhof, Louis. *Systematic Theology, New Combined Edition.* Grand Rapids, MI: W. B. Eerdmans Publishing Co.,1996, p.336.
3. Ibid, p.337.
4. Kubler-Ross, Elisabeth. *Wikipedia.org/wiki/Elisabeth.*
5. *Crucifixion of the King of Glory*, 109.
6. Lennox, John. "Why I Am I Christian" Youth Event in Perth, Australia.www.youtube.com/watch?v=jGrbrKWZFJg (last accessed 12/30/2025).
7. Cone, James H. *The Cross and the Lynching Tree.* Maryknoll, New *York:* Orbis Books, 2013.
8. Holman Study Bible NKJV Edition. Footnotes, 1095.

OTHER BOOKS BY THIS AUTHOR

Series 1: "Related Events to the Second Coming of the Christ."
Number of Books in the Series: 10

Vol.1

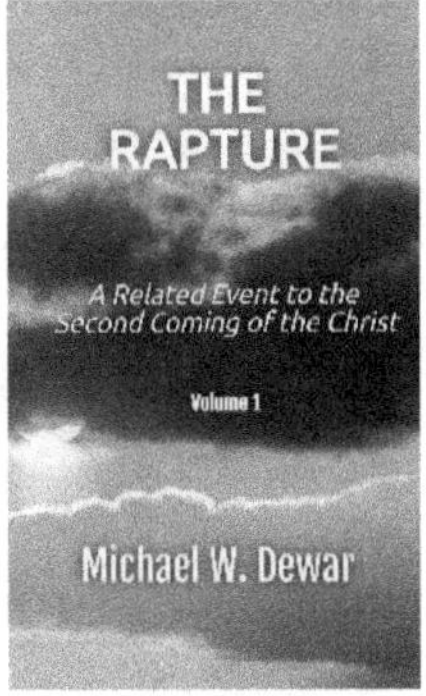

Vol.2

Vol.3

Vol. 4

Vol.5

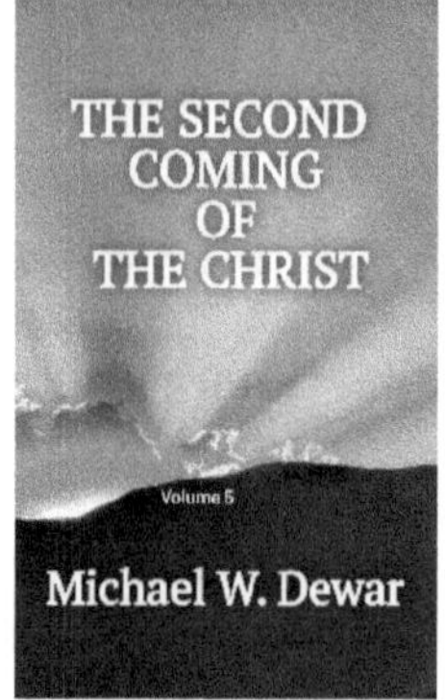

Vol.6

Vol.7

Vol.8

Vol.9

Vol.10

Series 2: Ready for the Coming Exodus? 3 Volumes. This series can be read in any order, but preferably as posted here.

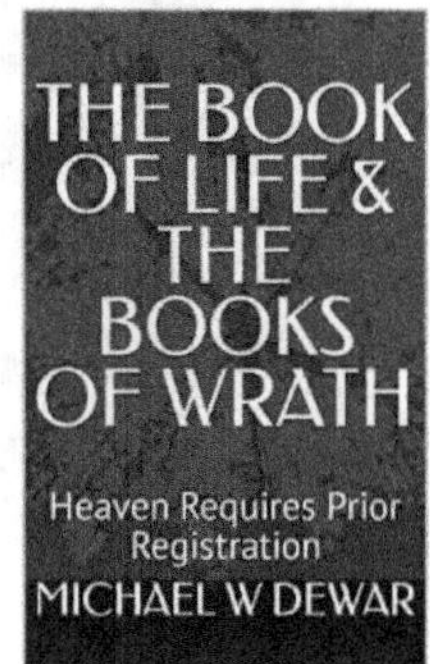

Series 3: *"Witnesses to an Execution."* 7 Volumes.

Vol.1

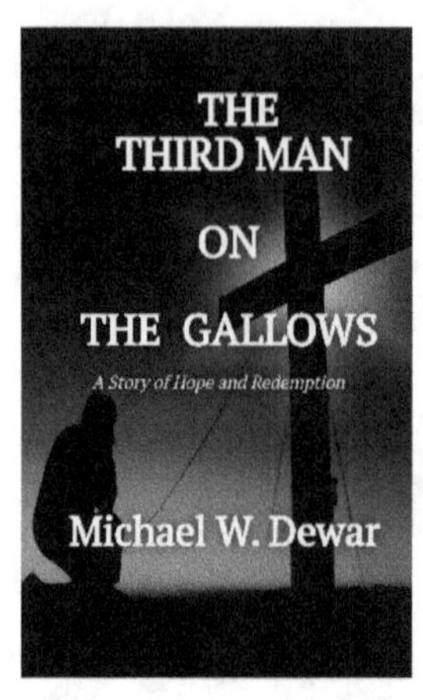

Vol. 2

Vol. 3

Vol.4

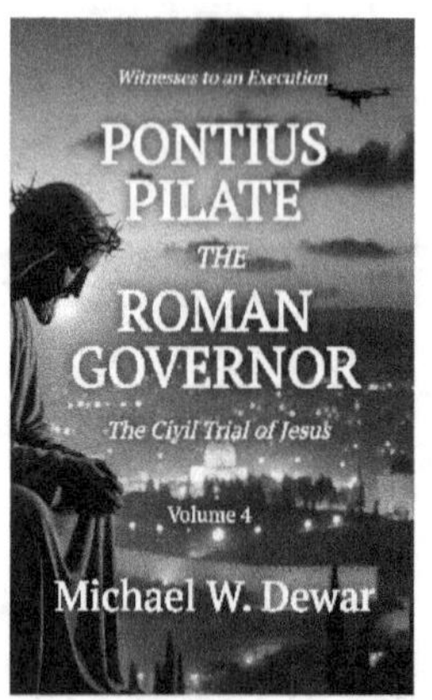

Vol.5

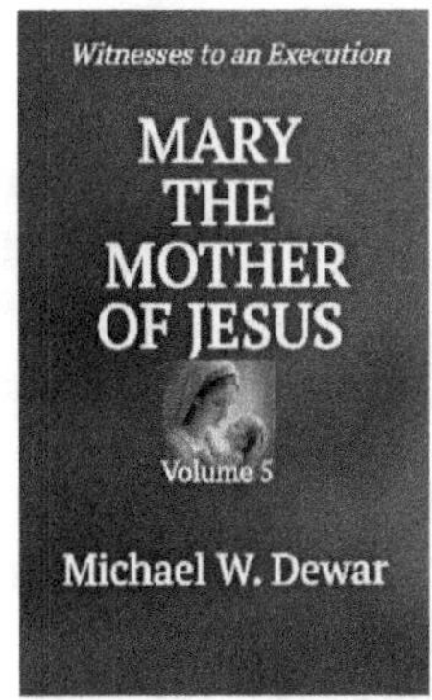

Vol.6

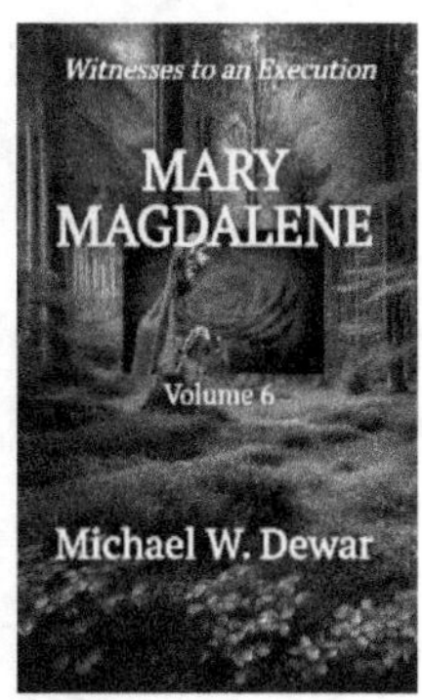

Vol.7

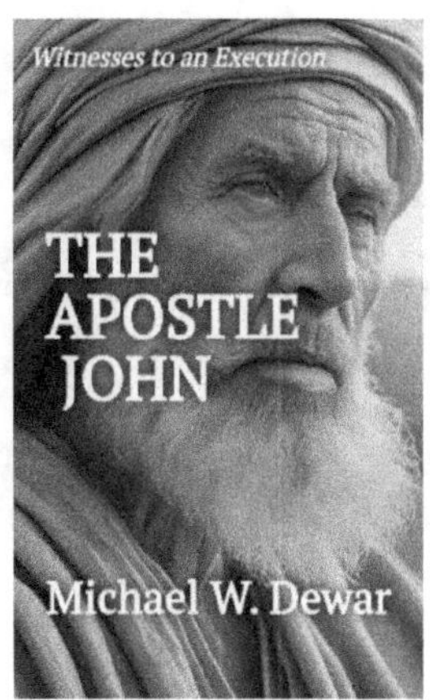

A STUDY IN THE RESOLUTION OF CONFLICTS

The following 3 Volumes constitute a course of Study in the Resolution of Conflict for local churches. Use them to launch a peace ministry in your local church. Become an Agent of Peace-Manager of Conflicts at your local church.

Textbook.

Instructor's Manual --- Students' Manual

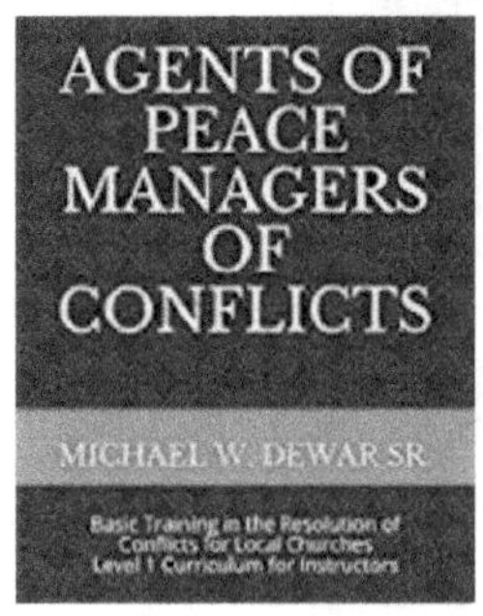

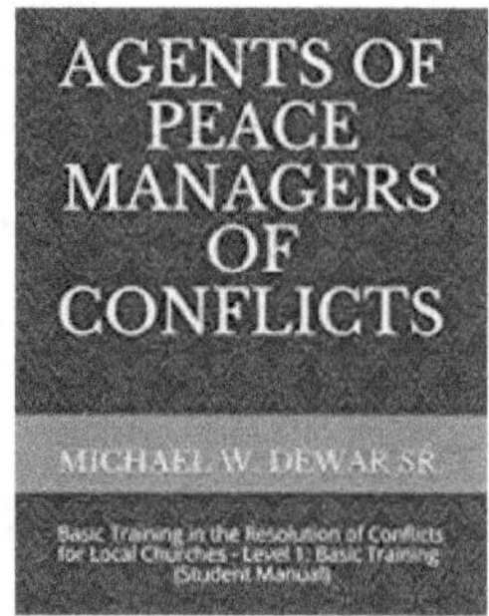

ABOUT THE AUTHOR

Michael W. Dewar, Sr. is a pastor, Bible teacher, and mentor in the spiritual life. He is also a specialist in the resolution of church and family conflicts. He authors a course of study for training Agents of Peace - Managers of Conflict for launching a peace ministry in local churches.

He holds earned degrees which includes, a B.A., the Master of Divinity, the Master of Social Work with License from the State of New York, and a doctorate. Rev. Dewar pastors in New York where he lives with his family.

Feedback Contacts:
Send feedback to the author at: **mdewar36@msn.com**
Or visit website at: dpscleansing.com or Dedwellingplace.com.